H.B. PHILLIPS
IMPRESARIO

'The grand old man of grand opera'
H.B. Phillips in 1948

H.B. PHILLIPS
impresario

THE MAN WHO BROUGHT McCORMACK,
KREISLER AND ROBESON TO DERRY

WESLEY McCANN

THE BELFAST SOCIETY
IN ASSOCIATION WITH
THE ULSTER HISTORICAL FOUNDATION

First published 2001
by the Belfast Society, c/o Linen Hall Library,
17 Donegall Square North, Belfast BT1 5GD
in association with the Ulster Historical Foundation
12 College Square East, Belfast BT1 6DD

Distributed by
the Ulster Historical Foundation

© Wesley McCann
ISBN 0-9539604-4-7

Printed by ColourBooks Ltd
Design by Dunbar Design

CONTENTS

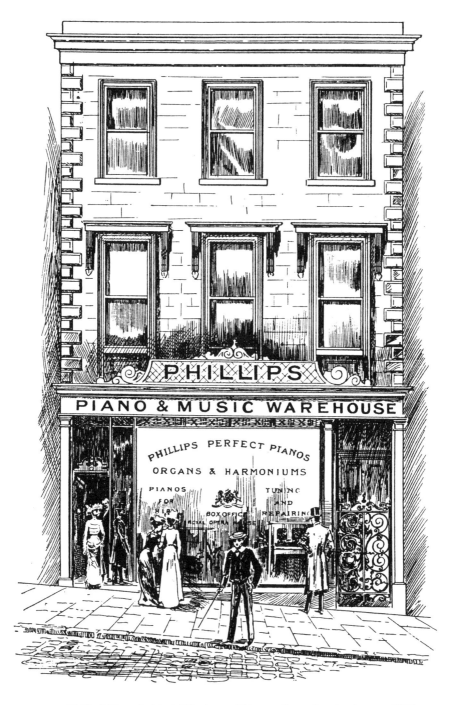

Phillips's Piano & Music Warehouse, Shipquay Street, Londonderry ca. 1900

INTRODUCTION

MOST STUDIES OF THE HISTORY OF MUSIC focus on composers, on their works and on those who perform them. Little attention has been paid to those who arrange for music to be performed. And yet without someone to choose a date and time, to hire a venue, book artists, display advertising, sell tickets, make sure the piano has been tuned and sort out the accounts and pay the bills, there would be no concerts for music lovers to enjoy. Often the efforts of promoters, agents and impresarios go unacknowledged and their names are known to only a few. As Norman Lebrecht has noted 'The existence of the main power-brokers in classical music is delicately ignored by major reference works …'.[1]

This brief study seeks to acknowledge the very considerable contribution to the musical life of Ireland and Great Britain by one such musical businessman who finds no place in any of the standard musical or biographical reference works.[2] From a beginning as a piano tuner in Londonderry[3] in the last decade of the nineteenth century Henry Bettesworth Phillips went on to promote concerts by many of the pre-eminent musicians of the day, to work (if only briefly) with the most dynamic young conductor in England, Thomas Beecham, and for the last third of his long life to own and run the country's principal touring opera company, the Carl Rosa. He brought live music to people and places which otherwise might never have had the chance to experience it, and he gave to performers – whether international superstars or those of more limited renown – the opportunity to appear before audiences throughout the length and breadth of the country.

This study had its origins in the finding in the Public Record Office of Northern Ireland of a file of correspondence relating to three concerts promoted in Derry in the 1930s, which led to a desire to discover more about the man behind them.[4] Very early in my researches I had the very good fortune to be put in touch with members of the family of H.B. Phillips and without their generous assistance and encouragement I could not have achieved even this modest account of their forebear. In particular I wish to acknowledge the help given me by H.B. Phillips's son Ian Henry 'Peter' Phillips who sadly died before my work was completed; his own sons Anthony and Robin who have answered many questions and shared with me their recollections and knowledge of their grandparents; Mrs Kathleen Hobson, H.B. Phillips's niece, who kindly received me in her home and allowed me to see the autograph album and other memorabilia kept by her uncle; and lastly Mrs Maureen Phillips who married into the Phillips family and helped run the Derry side of the business until it closed. Her knowledge of her adopted family has been invaluable to me, and when she learnt of my interest in Phillips she readily shared with me the documentation and information she had assembled over many years.

Others have helped me in all sorts of ways and it is a pleasure to record their names here as a token of my gratitude to them: Mrs Maura Craig of Derry Central Library; Mrs Linda Greenwood of Belfast Central Library; Mr Ulrich Gerhartz of Steinway and Sons, London; Mr Ian St John Jones; Mr Nat McGlinchy; Mr Sean Nolan; Ms Bridget Palmer of the Royal Academy of Music, London; Mr Alan Roberts of the Foyle College Old Boys' Association; the staffs of the Linen Hall Library, Belfast, the Public Record Office of Northern Ireland, and the British Library, London. I am grateful to my colleagues Charles Reid and Ann Cairns for help with the information technology which makes the writer's task so much easier. Lastly it is a pleasure to acknowledge the helpful advice of Amber Adams and Angélique Day, and my gratitude to the Belfast Society for accepting this study for publication.

In all other respects I remain responsible for the work, and for any errors, omissions or infelicities of style I take full responsibility.

WESLEY McCANN
STRANMILLIS UNIVERSITY COLLEGE BELFAST
OCTOBER, 2001

NOTES

1   NORMAN LEBRECHT, *When the music stops: managers, maestros and the corporate murder of classical music* (London: Simon & Schuster, 1996), p. 5.

2   Among those works which make no mention of him are the *Dictionary of national biography* (and there are no plans to include him in the *New DNB*), *The new Grove dictionary of music and musicians*, 2nd edition (London: Macmillan, 2001) – save for a passing reference in the entry for the opera company he owned; HENRY BOYLAN, *A dictionary of Irish biography*, 3rd edition (Dublin: Gill and Macmillan, 1998), and KATE NEWMANN, *Dictionary of Ulster biography* (Belfast: Institute of Irish Studies, 1993).

3   Like most natives of Northern Ireland I have used the names Londonderry and Derry interchangeably, other than in quotations and proper titles.

4   Public Record Office of Northern Ireland [hereafter PRONI] D3497/1.

Shipquay Street, Londonderry in the early years of the twentieth century.
A group of passers-by look into the large plate glass window of Phillips's shop.
Beyond the city gate can be seen the clock tower of the Guildhall.

AUTHOR'S COLLECTION

1

FROM CHORISTER
TO IMPRESARIO

THE LIFE AND TIMES OF
HENRY BETTESWORTH PHILLIPS

ORIGINS

HENRY BETTESWORTH PHILLIPS was born in Athy, Co Kildare[1] on 23 December 1866, the third child of Henry St John Phillips and his wife Jane. Henry St John was the fifth son of James Phillips, originally of Fethard in Co. Tipperary, but later resident in Dublin. He and Jane, daughter of William Jervis Lawless, a jeweller and silversmith of Rose Inn Street Kilkenny[2], were married in St Mary's Parish Church Kilkenny on 6 August 1863. They had ten children in all, the eldest being a daughter, Jane, born in April 1864. A son, William Henry died at six months leaving Henry Bettesworth as the oldest boy.[3] He had six younger brothers, all of whom, with one exception, survived to adulthood, and a younger sister who died at the age of three. His father, who was thirty years old at the time of Henry's birth, is variously described in the birth certificates of his children as a stationmaster, watchmaker and jeweller, or, on occasion, 'gentleman'.[4]

The Phillips family were members of the Church of Ireland, and Henry St John is named in the street directory for 1870 as secretary to the Young Men's Christian Association in Kilkenny.[5] His involvement in the YMCA, a socially-minded evangelical movement founded in London in 1844 and which soon had branches throughout Britain, Ireland and beyond, suggests a Christian commitment which was more than merely nominal.

Henry St John Phillips died on 18 March 1879 at the compara-
tively early age of 43 leaving his widow with a daughter and seven
sons to care for; the oldest, Henry Bettesworth, not yet thirteen, and
the youngest, George ffolliott, barely eighteen months old.

EDUCATION

According to several of his obituary notices Henry had, by age of ten
(i.e. in about 1876 or 1877), won a scholarship as a boy soloist in the
choir of the Church of Ireland (Anglican) Cathedral in Londonderry.[6]
Why his parents should have chosen to send him north to Derry is
not readily apparent unless it was to take advantage of the scholarship.
So far as is known neither side of their extended family had any connection with the city, but whatever the reason, it was to Derry that
Henry went and there he completed his schooling and began to make
his way in the world.

St Columb's Cathedral in Londonderry had been built in 1633 by
the Honourable the Irish Society of the City Corporation of London
as part of the rebuilding of the city laid waste in the insurrections of
the previous seventy years. An example of Planter's or Ulster gothic,
by the late nineteenth century the building had been much altered,
but, with the exception of the chancel and an extra bay to the east
added in 1885, the Cathedral today looks much as it did in Henry's
time.[7] At the date when Henry is said to have joined the choir the
dean of the Cathedral was the Reverend Charles Seymour DD who
had taken up the post in 1874 and held it until his death in 1882 at
the age of sixty. He is described as being 'of the Evangelical party, not
very learned, but very pious and much respected'.[8] If the dean were
thought not very learned (despite his doctorate in divinity) the same
could not be said of the man who had been bishop of the diocese
since 1867, William Alexander, later (1896) Archbishop of Armagh.
Educated at Oxford and a renowned preacher and the author of many
works of scholarship, Bishop Alexander was the first native of Derry
to be appointed to the see.[9] His wife Cecil Frances Alexander was the
celebrated hymn writer.[10]

By the 1870s the musical life of the Cathedral was beginning
to show signs of improvement after a long period of low standards
and unsatisfactory performance. The middle years of the nineteenth

century found the organ in a 'deranged state', and in 1873 £228 was spent on repairs.[11] Before the addition of the chancel the organ stood at the west end of the building while the choir sat at the opposite end, an arrangement which made accompanying the singing particularly difficult.[12] The organist when Henry joined the choir was James Turpin, and the 'job description' issued to candidates applying to succeed him when he left in 1878 shows a pattern of worship based firmly on the Book of Common Prayer. Services were sung on Sundays and at Morning Prayer each Wednesday, as well as 'on those days throughout the year for which a gospel and epistle are appointed', that is the saints days and other festivals in the Prayer Book. The organist was required to give five hours each week to training the choir of men, boys and girls. The situation was summarised as 'musical but not full cathedral', by which it was presumably meant that sung services were not held every day and that the singing was restricted to hymns, psalms and an anthem from the standard repertory of that time.[13] Turpin was succeeded by Daniel C. Jones of Lichfield who was to hold the post until his death in 1911.[14] Jones was accompanied to Derry by his younger brother Robert who was soon appointed organist of St Augustine's Church in the city. In January 1885 Robert became Henry Phillips's brother in law when he married his older sister Jane who had moved with the family from Kilkenny to Derry.[15]

However limited the musical endeavours of the Cathedral it no doubt provided young Henry with a thorough grounding in the rudiments of music, and he rose to become the head boy in the choir. On Christmas Eve 1881 he took the solo soprano rôle in a performance of the first part of Handel's *Messiah* given in the Cathedral under the direction of the organist. A report of the performance in a local newspaper commented that he had a 'voice of extraordinary sweetness and compass, and when to this is coupled a keen appreciation of the requirements of the music, the result may be easily imagined'.[16]

It is probable that he first attended the Cathedral's Infant School which in 1870 was under the direction of the Mistress Mary Mooney and her assistant Lizzie Wilson,[17] and on 6 September 1879 Henry was enrolled as a pupil in Foyle College, Londonderry.[18] Founded in 1617 and called at first the Free School, Foyle College was the name by which it had been known since its move to new premises in 1814. The Headmaster was Maurice Charles Hime, a graduate of Trinity

College, Dublin who before moving to Foyle had been for eleven years headmaster of the Diocesan School in Monaghan.[19] He was appointed in 1877 but did not take up the post until the following year. The school was at rather a low ebb and Hime seems to have been brought in to improve matters. One of his first acts was the issuing of a *Prospectus* setting out his four-fold objectives for the 'the sons of gentlemen' under his care:

> (1)To develop the Religious and Moral; (2) the Intellectual; and (3) the Physical powers of the boys; while (4) the most careful attention is paid to their manners and address.[20]

To emphasise the religious and moral foundation of school life family prayers were said twice each day and the boys attended divine worship in the Cathedral or a nearby church on Sunday mornings. A college service was held in the evening when hymns were sung 'one of the Masters or boys playing the accompaniment on the harmonium' (*Prospectus*, p. 3). These devotions were supplemented by regular lectures by the local clergy and by biblical and catechetical instruction.

The intellectual side of the boys' development was provided for in a curriculum which included Latin and Greek, composition, literature, history, mathematics, French, German and book-keeping, the latter being of particular importance in a system which was aimed at providing 'a commercial and middle class education'. With the exception of those who were specially prepared for university, civil service or military examinations Dr Hime knew that most of his boys were destined for a life in business. No specific mention is made of musical tuition in the *Prospectus*, although it is listed as an extra for which a guinea and a half per quarter was charged. A list of the principal members of staff in about 1880 names two music teachers: P. Mulholland, organist of St Eugene's Roman Catholic Cathedral and D.C. Jones from St Columb's.[21] An earlier directory specifically named a piano teacher, John Horan, and a bandmaster, Herr Stoll, all of which suggests a lively musical tradition in the school.[22]

The physical side of the boys' development was provided for in football, cricket and riding, and the school boasted a 'very good ball-alley, an excellent gymnasium, a fly-pole[23] and a large cricket and foot-ball field' (*Prospectus*, p. 3). A list of fourteen rules governed the boys' behaviour, including 'That each boy before going to dinner hang up his cap or hat and great coat in their proper place, wash his hands and face, brush his hair, etc.', and 'That no boy keep his hands in his trousers' pockets' (*Prospectus*, pp. 5–6).

As the majority of boys were boarders much emphasis was placed on the importance of letters home. To encourage the boys to develop a good compositional style each Monday they were required to write a 'composition letter' to a parent or friend which was marked as an ordinary lesson, 'the folding of the letter, its general neatness, the address and position of the stamp on the envelope, being taken into consideration as well as the style, the spelling, and length of the composition itself' (*Prospectus*, p. 7). All of these were skills which a young man entering the world of commerce would find invaluable. Seventy years later, after a lifetime of writing innumerable business letters, Henry's hand still showed evidence of having been well formed and his correspondence, though often hastily written, was both legible and clearly set out. He had learned the lessons of the schoolroom well.

Fees for boarders at Foyle College were 54 guineas per annum with reduction for brothers and the sons of clergymen (*Prospectus*, p. 4). Day boys over the age of ten were charged 10 guineas for a modern education (that is, without Latin and Greek) and twelve for a classical one (*Prospectus*, p. 43).

By modern standards the school system might appear severe and inflexible, but in one respect the Headmaster was well ahead of his time: he totally rejected the use of corporal punishment, a rejection founded on both moral and pragmatic grounds:

> The Head-master is convinced that any kind of corporal punishment is (1) debasing and injurious to the scholastic profession in general; (2) is degrading to the Schoolmaster who inflicts it, it being calculated to deaden the best affections and blunt the finest feelings of his nature; and (3) that it is both a useless and mischievous mode of punishment, as far as the boys on whom it is inflicted are concerned (*Prospectus*, p. 14).

The physical environment of the school was also an enlightened one. The years 1877 and 1878 had seen the extensive renovation of all the rooms and the installation of hot and cold running water and gas lighting. The surgeon to the City and County of Derry Infirmary, Sir William Millar, appended a report to the *Prospectus* in which he attested to the high quality of the water supply and ventilation, the efficient sewerage and the overall high standards of the school buildings (*Prospectus*, p. 14).

In 1878, the year before Henry joined the school, one of the music masters, Mr Mulholland, set to music some words written by 'a poetic friend' at the request of the Headmaster. One wonders if they struck a chord with the new boy entering the school at a time of considerable optimism under a new headmaster and in much improved accommodation:

> O good old school that stands in pride
> Above the winding Foyle,
> Made dear by days of mirth and play
> And days of hopeful toil,
> Though half in fear we first drew near
> Your halls of ancient fame,
> We've learnt to love you, dear old school,
> And glory in your name.
> Then shirk, lads, no work, lads,
> But strive with might and main,
> To guard the fame her sons have won,
> Undimmed by blot or stain.[24]

DERRY IN THE 1870S

The city which was to be Henry's home for the next thirty odd years and in which he was to maintain a business interest for the rest of his life was a city undergoing rapid change.[25] From the time of the rebuilding of the city in 1614 until the opening years of the nineteenth century Londonderry had remained a protestant city within the confines of the city walls. But with the coming of the new century its population began to grow and change as more and more people, many of them Roman Catholics from the Inishowen peninsula in Co Donegal, began to settle outside the walls. Here there grew up the denominationally-divided communities which were united only in the squalor and poverty in which they lived. By the middle of the 1830s Roman Catholics made up almost half the city's population of 19,000 and by 1851 they were in the majority, although control of the city's affairs remained in protestant hands (apart from one brief interlude) for more than a century to come. Not surprisingly the change in the religious and political makeup of the population brought with it a growth in tension which often resulted in civil unrest.

As the population grew so did the economic life of the city, and the shirt industry for which Derry became famous throughout the world was established in the 1830s. For a time shipbuilding prospered, and, as one of the most westerly ports in Europe, Derry became an important centre for trade with North America. Part of that trade was in emigrants who increased in number after the famine years of 1845-6. The 1840s and 50s saw the coming of the railways linking Derry to the other major towns of the north of Ireland.

By the time of young Henry's arrival in the city in 1876 the population had grown to over 26,000 of whom 10,000 were employed in the shirt industry. The majority of these were women mostly working at home as 'outworkers', making up the component parts of the shirts supplied to them by the factories. In the closing decades of the century political tension rose further mainly focused then, as now, on the right to hold marches to celebrate the events of the siege of the city in 1689.

EARLY SUCCESSES

The growth in size and prosperity of the city brought with it a middle class with the money and inclination to indulge in music and other cultural pastimes, and responding to these needs was to provide a career and a living for Henry when, in 1882 in his fifteenth year, he left Foyle College.[26] Thereafter he served an apprenticeship at one of the music business in Derry and also spent some time 'extending his experience with a leading London house of piano manufacturers' before setting up in business on his own account probably in 1890 or 1891. This is claimed in a publication intended to promote and advertise the commercial life of the city.[27] It boasted on his behalf that his 'well appointed piano and music saloon [sic] is one of the most popular establishments in Derry'. It is often the case in publications of this type that the entry is written by the subject himself so a certain exaggeration might have to be allowed for, but it is clear that his business was growing rapidly. Unfortunately neither of the firms with which he served an apprenticeship is named but Derry had by this time a number of thriving musical businesses.[28] The earliest listing in the street directory dates from1892 and has him trading as a piano tuner and dealer in Marlborough Street in Derry.[29]

The 1890s saw the beginning of the pre-eminence of the piano as the source of music making in the home, and by the end of the nineteenth century world production had increased tenfold. The quality of manufacture of even a modestly priced instrument had improved enormously and the cost was within the means of a teacher or clerk.[30] The supply and maintenance of pianos was to be a major part of H.B. Phillips's business for many years to come.[31]

On 8 October 1891 Henry Phillips promoted his first major concert. It was no merely provincial affair but an event which brought to the city one of the leading European virtuosi of the day. The venue was the Guildhall, Derry's newest and most prestigious building, erected at a cost of £20,000 and opened in 1890. It at once became, and has remained, the city's principal concert location.[32] A newspaper report described the concert as the building's 'musical baptism' and commented that 'no audience more brilliant or appreciative has yet assembled at a concert within the Guildhall.'[33] The artist they had come to enjoy was Tivadar Nachez (1859–1932), a Hungarian-born violinist who settled in London and enjoyed a highly successful career as a soloist. The local reporter was in no doubt as to his eminence and the good fortune of the people of Londonderry in being able to hear him in their magnificent new hall:

> The opportunity of hearing a violinist who has been feted by Royalty in nearly every country in the world, and who appeared wearing several decorations from foreign Courts, is rarely within the reach of provincial audiences. Thursday night's concert, in fact, was one of those which go towards placing the provinces on terms of equality with the metropolis in regard to musical lions such as Nachez, who has been spoken of as the successor in point of genius of Paginini. That the rarety [sic] of the occasion and the excellence of the treat provided were thoroughly recognised was evidenced in the fact that the hall was crowded to its very doors. The concert will long remain as a delightful reminiscence of the opening of the present season.

The report concludes with a generous acknowledgement of Phillips's achievement in bringing Nachez to the city:

> Mr H.B. Phillips, to whose enterprise the organising of the concert

was due, may be congratulated on the splendid result of his initial venture, which, we are gratified to learn, he intends following up before long.

When it is recalled that Phillips was not yet twenty-five years old the achievement is all the more noteworthy, but, as will become apparent, throughout his career he displayed a flair for pulling off the big event and he had no difficulty in persuading the biggest names in the business to come to Ireland and to his adopted city.

Other promotions followed, not only in Londonderry but farther afield. In Omagh in March 1892 Phillips organised a ballad concert, for which he also supplied a Bechstein piano, and in October of the same year he put on a concert in Armagh featuring the celebrated Welsh tenor Ben Davies.[34] These promotions were undertaken from his premises in Marlborough Street, but from the evidence of the street directory by 1896 he had moved to Union Buildings.[35] By 1899 he had taken up occupation of 30 Shipquay Street,[36] at which address, under the name 'Beethoven House', the firm he established remained one of the city's best known businesses until 1980.[37] By December 1899 he was promoting concerts in Belfast,[38] and on 18 April 1902 he brought there the most famous English contralto of her day, Clara Butt, together with her husband, the baritone Kennerley Rumford. [39] These concerts were given in the Wellington Hall, the headquarters of the YMCA in the city. Clara Butt, later Dame Clara, and Rumford were to visit Ireland on a number of other occasions under Phillips's direction.

As if running a piano and music shop and promoting concerts were not enough, in October 1896 Phillips took control of the Derry Opera House. Opened in August 1877 it was owned and run by the English actor and manager Joseph F. Warden. In December 1895 Warden opened the Grand Opera House in Belfast and thereafter concentrated his business interests there.[40] (He already owned the Theatre Royal in Belfast.) Phillips continued to run the Derry Opera House until 1903 and provided a mixed fare of drama, opera and operetta.

In 1904 Henry Bettesworth Phillips married Annette Prior, daughter of Henry M. Prior, an apothecary long-established in business at 7 Ferryquay Street in Derry.[41] Nettie (as she was known) was Henry's junior by fourteen years and an accomplished pianist. She studied piano and harmony at the Royal Academy of Music in London, entering in January 1899 and awarded the Licentiate (LRAM) in the following year.[42] While studying in London she lived with her older sister Ethel who was married to a Harley Street doctor, Fancourt Banes.[43] Among the Phillips Papers is the programme of a concert given by the distinguished Scottish baritone Andrew Black in Newry in January 1904 in which Miss Nettie Prior played a number of solo works for piano as well as accompanying the violinist Miss Ernestine MacCormack.

Henry and Nettie's daughter Ailne (known to her family as Babs) was born in Derry on 5 June 1905, and a second child, Ian Henry (known as Peter), was born to them in 1914 following their move to England. Nettie continued her professional career for a time after the birth of her daughter and appeared as an accompanist in a concert in Belfast in December 1908,[44] and in October 1909 played at a concert given by John McCormack in Derry.[45] Later she was to work closely with her husband in his business ventures. Babs enjoyed a distinguished career as a ballet dancer and teacher, most notably with the Carl Rosa Opera Company and with the late Dame Ninette de Valois at Sadlers Wells Ballet, later the Royal Ballet.[46] She died in 1992.

BELFAST

In 1907 H.B. Phillips opened a second shop, this time in Belfast, and it was there that his activities as a concert agent were concentrated in the years leading up to the First World War.[47] His premises were located at nos 2–4 Bedford Street, within a hundred yards of the Ulster Hall, the principal concert venue in the city. The shop, which, like the one in Derry, he named 'Beethoven House', was on a prominent corner site in an imposing building erected only a few years earlier.[48] It looked out on Belfast's 'exuberant Edwardian wedding-cake of a city hall in Portland stone' which had been opened in the previous year.[49]

The shop stocked a range of pianos including two of the leading makes for which Phillips was the sole agent – Broadwood and Blüthner – together with a less expensive model, 'Phillips Perfect Pianos', priced from only £21. The piano was one of the first household items to be sold by hire purchase,[50] and Phillips offered a range of instruments under the 'three year system'.[51] A £21 piano could be had for twelve payments of £2 per quarter and, what was more, came with a ten-year guarantee.[52] In addition he offered the 'Finest Stock of Sheet Music in the North of Ireland', 'Violins, Strings, Fittings, Tunings', and 'Repairs by Competent Workmen'. He also advertised the 'Beethoven House Band' which was available for hire for 'At Homes and Dances'.[53] By 1909 Phillips had opened a 'Gramophone Salon', expanding into the premises next door to make room for it.[54] The salon offered a wide range of models ranging from the 'Victor Monarch' at £3 10s 0d to the 'Junior Grand' in mahogany at £15 0s 0d, as well as all the latest gramophone records as they were released.[55]

Phillips was an advocate of the latest technology, and his shop stocked both the 'Electrelle', a 'wonderful invention that fits into any piano, permits the performance of any music, and is capable of complete artistic expression and individualism', and the 'Auxetophone', a device for amplifying the sound of a gramophone. Both were used in a concert in the Ulster Hall on 24 November 1909, one of many such events at that time which combined live artists and the recorded performances of others.[56]

It was however as a promoter of concerts that Phillips made his greatest contribution to the musical life of Belfast and the rest of Ireland at this time. He ran two series of concerts; 'Phillips Subscription Concerts', and 'Phillips Dublin, Belfast, and Irish Provincial Concerts'. The elaborate, multi-coloured programme cover for the latter series named eighteen towns and cities throughout Ireland along with Belfast and Dublin, although it is doubtful if he regularly promoted concerts in some of the smaller centres. Many of the world's leading artists were included in these series, some returning several times.

One of the first concerts, on 10 December 1907, featured the Hallé Orchestra under Hans Richter. The Hallé, established in Manchester in 1858 as Britain's first professional orchestra, had in Richter Europe's leading conductor to direct them. He had been appointed conductor of the Hallé in 1899 after almost a quarter of a century directing the Vienna Philharmonic Orchestra. He was a great champion of the music of the then little-known Edward Elgar, and conducted the first performances of the *Enigma variations*, *The Dream of Gerontius* and the composer's first symphony.[57] The Hallé had been to Belfast several times before under a different promoter and Richter had conducted them there in November 1899 and in March 1900.[58]

Autograph of Hans Richter, Belfast 10 December 1907.
This was his third visit to the city and the first under Phillips's direction.
The music is that of the opening bars of the works performed.

The programme in December 1907 included substantial fare: Beethoven's Symphony no 4, two overtures by Wagner, and Richard Strauss's symphonic poem *Til Eulenspiegel*. [59] Although the Ulster Hall was not well filled one of the morning newspapers was generous in its praise of Phillips for bringing the orchestra to the city and expressed the hope that he would do so again.[60] Phillips did arrange for two further visits of Richter and the Hallé, on 26 March 1909, and again on 17 March 1911. This St Patrick's Day concert was part of Richter's farewell tour with the Orchestra; he gave his last performance with them in Huddersfield less than a fortnight later on 28 March.[61] His final appearance in Belfast was billed as a 'Plebiscite Programme', its contents having been 'chosen by Mr Phillips's subscribers'. Not surprisingly, knowing the conductor's reputation as an interpreter of Wagner (he had worked with the composer and given first performances of several of his operas), the audience had requested both the overture to *Tannhauser* and the prelude and closing scene from *Tristan*. They also chose Beethoven's Symphony no 7 and works by Liszt, Saint-Saëns and Brahms.[62] A postcard sent by Richter to his friend Percy Pitt in London has survived which provides colourful background to his visit to Belfast. Dated 17 March and written in German the translation reads:

> Columbus, Vasco da Gama and all sea-farers of former periods were land lubbers compared with me: I crossed in a steamer from Liverpool to Belfast without being sick – Today St Patrick is being celebrated with terrific uproar; already – 10.30am – some part-hic-ularly [sic] active worshippers of St Whiskus are gathering in the streets.[63]

Phillips was to bring the Hallé to Belfast on other occasions: on 29 March 1912 when it was conducted by Sir Henry Wood, best remembered as the driving force behind the Promenade Concerts,[64] and on 1 April 1913 and again on 4 March 1914 under the baton of Hamilton Harty, the Ulster-born composer and conductor who was no stranger to Ulster Hall audiences.[65]

Whereas the Hallé was a long-established orchestra and Richter was nearing the end of his distinguished career, Thomas Beecham and his orchestra, which Phillips brought to Belfast on 25 October 1909, were just embarking on a career which was to have a huge impact on the musical life of the country.[66] The twenty-nine year old Beecham had formed his symphony orchestra in 1909 and recruited to it some of the finest players in London. He undertook an extensive tour of Britain and Ireland in October 1909, beginning in Exeter and working northwards until crossing to Ireland for the concert in Belfast and another in Dublin on the following day.[67] At each venue the programme included Elgar's first symphony which had been given its première (under Richter) in December of the previous year. The inclusion of the work is somewhat surprising as Beecham had an ambivalent attitude towards it and saw fit to abbreviate it in his own way. He managed to reduce a work of 55 minutes' duration to a mere 38, declaring 'I don't know how it sounds, and I don't care!'[68] Other works in the programme included Smetana's overture to the *Bartered Bride*, the overture to *The Wreckers* by the English composer Ethel Smyth whom Beecham did much to promote, and Debussy's *Prélude à l'après-midi d'un faune*.[69]

As well as bringing the finest orchestras and conductors to Ireland Phillips gave audiences the opportunity to enjoy some of the most notable soloists of the day. The violinists Ysäye (4 February 1908), Kubelik (2 November 1910), and Kreisler (25 November 1910 and 20 October 1911), the pianist Busoni (14 February 1913), the singers Clara Butt and Kennerley Rumford (14 April 1910 and 5 May 1911) and the Irish tenor John McCormack (7 October 1910 and 11 October 1912) all graced the stage of the Ulster Hall. But his greatest achievement at this time took place on 15 September 1909 when he brought the most celebrated artist of the age to Belfast – Enrico Caruso.

Autograph and self portrait of Caruso on the occasion of his visit to Belfast 1909. Caruso was famous for these rapid sketches which capture perfectly his robust build.

PHILLIPS PAPERS

CARUSO

Belfast was one of ten venues on a tour of Britain and Ireland begun in Dublin on 20 August and ending in Liverpool a month later undertaken by the great tenor, and it was the only tour which Caruso made to the provinces in a career which spanned the period 1895 to 1920. [70] By the date of the visit he had already made over 100 recordings and his voice would have been well known to many in the audience. Phillips must have expected that the chance to see the great man in the flesh would create an unprecedented demand for tickets. So spectacular a coup was his visit that the prospectus Phillips issued referred to the whole season as the 'Caruso Season' and prices were raised accordingly. The most expensive seats were priced at 21 shillings (twice that charged for the Beecham concert), and the cheapest were three times dearer at 7s 6d. This was at a time when a ton of Scotch coal or a new set of false teeth could be had in Belfast for 21 shillings, and five cigars cost only a shilling. However, Phillips was careful to point out that in Edinburgh the front seats to hear Caruso cost a staggering 31s 6d.[71]

But at such high prices sales were at first slow and almost forty years later Phillips recalled a singular act of generosity by a Belfast businessman:

> I remember when I had Caruso in the Ulster Hall Alec Carlisle (Harland & Wolff) bought 500 tickets at a reduced rate & gave them to the workers. This was after he saw the plan was not too well booked.[72]

Alexander Montgomery Carlisle was the managing director of the world famous shipbuilding firm and a great lover of music.[73] The work force of Harland & Wolff at the time numbered in excess of 10,000 and it is not known how the lucky five hundred were chosen.

As the concert drew nearer Phillips used all his skill as a promoter to work up a fever of anticipation and to push sales right up to the last moment. On the preceding day an advertisement in the local press breathlessly announced that '600 people were turned away at Glasgow. There are still a few seats left for Wednesday Night's Concert. Immediate application imperative'.[74] On the morning of the concert another advertisement declared 'Caruso has arrived and will sing tonight'.[75] It went on to give detailed instructions to ticket holders about which entrance to use (all of which created an expectation of thronging crowds), and promised that a few unreserved seats would be sold at the door. The concert was to commence 'as soon after 8 o'clock as the audience is seated'. In the same newspaper Phillips's name appeared with two other gramophone dealers, T.E. Osborne of Donegall Square West and Smyth & Co of Donegall Street, in an exceptionally large advertisement taken by The Gramophone Company proclaiming:

CARUSO IS SINGING IN BELFAST TO-DAY.
If you are unable to attend his Concert,
or if having done so you desire to recall
the exquisite sensations you experience, the
GRAMOPHONE
will bring to your home the living voice not only of
CARUSO
but of all the World's Greatest Artistes.

On the afternoon of his visit Caruso was entertained to lunch by A.M. Carlisle and his fellow directors and given a tour of the ship-building yard. No doubt he would have been shown the keel of Titanic which had been laid only a few months earlier. Elsewhere in the city the enterprising Northern Motor Company in its premises behind the Ulster Hall proclaimed itself the 'Caruso Concert Garage' and offered parking for a shilling. The concert was a huge success and the *Belfast Newsletter* in acknowledging Phillips's enterprise in bringing Caruso to Belfast reported that:

> Many famous tenors have sung in the Ulster Hall, but one cannot recall any of them who was quite so perfect in voice, feeling, and power as this serious-looking Neapolitan, whose passionate earnestness is reflected in his voice, as well as the firm lines of his large round face.[76]

In all, Phillips's many concerts in the period before 1914 were among the most brilliant ever promoted in Ireland, and when set alongside the wide range of concerts promoted by the Belfast Philharmonic Society[77] and other amateur music societies, they show that this was indeed a golden age for the Belfast music lover. Although the gramophone was beginning to claim a growing share of the music market the live event was still the choice of the majority, and in the Ulster Hall, Belfast had one of the largest and finest concert venues in Britain and Ireland.[78]

WORKING FOR BEECHAM

Perhaps because of the association with Beecham formed when the latter brought his orchestra to Belfast in 1909, three years later Phillips found himself working as General Manager of the Thomas Beecham Opera, Symphony Orchestra, and Wind Orchestra. This at any rate is how he described himself in an advertisement in the programme for a concert in his 'Dublin, Belfast and Irish Provincial Concerts' series on 11 October 1912 featuring McCormack and others.[79] The advertisement mentions Beecham's forthcoming Covent Garden season beginning on 27 January 1913[80] which was to include the first performance in England of Richard Strauss's best-known opera *Rosenkavalier*. It also publicised the Russian Ballet at the same venue, and a forthcoming Paris Season during the month of June

1913 when *Rosenkavalier* and another of Strauss's operas, *Elektra*, would be given there for the first time.[81] Lastly the advertisement looked forward to the visit of the Beecham Orchestra (in November and December 1912) to the Royal Opera House Kroll, Berlin.[82] All this was to take place under the management of H.B. Phillips whose address was given as 17 Orchard Street, Portman Square, London. The Russian Ballet Russe was of course under the direction of Serge Diaghilev whose company took Europe by storm in 1911 and changed the face of twentieth-century ballet forever.

Surviving from this period is a letter from Phillips to Richter written on behalf of the Beecham Opera Company. The letterhead gives Phillips's name and the Orchard Street address and proclaims his management of Kreisler, John McCormack and Beecham. Dated 20 November 1912 it is addressed to Richter in Bayreuth where he had settled on his retirement.

Dear Dr. Richter,

As no doubt you have heard that Mr Thomas Beecham is giving an opera season at Covent Garden, commencing on Jan. 27th when he proposes doing the "Rosenkavalier", "Salome", "Elektra", "The Meistersinger" and "Tristan". The performances of the "Meistersinger" take place on Feb. 24th, 26th, March 3rd and 5th; and I write to see if you could come over and conduct one or two performances, and if so what your fee would be.

Hoping you are in good health, and enjoying your well-earned rest.

Believe me,
Yours very sincerely,
[signed] Henry B Phillips[83]

As Phillips had brought Richter to Belfast on a number of occasions he doubtless hoped for a positive reply, but Richter, who had already given the final performance of his long career on 19 August 1912,[84] turned the letter over and wrote on the back to Percy Pitt (managing director of Covent Garden and later first director of music at the BBC). Richter made no attempt to hide his disdain of Beecham: 'I have refused this invitation. So the pill-father seems to support the undertakings of the son.'[85] The reference is to the Beecham family fortune which came from the sale of digestive pills first produced by Sir Thomas's grandfather and developed to a world-wide business by his father Joseph who underwrote the costs of many of Thomas's ambitious musical ventures. Beecham made a second direct approach to Richter early in 1913, but again Richter refused.[86] Relations between Richter and Beecham were never good. Beecham regarded the illustrious Austro-Hungarian as an obstacle to his own advancement,[87] and perhaps it was this snub by Richter which prompted Beecham to write of him in his autobiography some thirty years later: 'In those days [ie when Richter conducted the Hallé] he enjoyed a commanding prestige which owed more to his personal association with Richard Wagner than to a talent which had decided limitations. A few things he interpreted admirably, a great many more indifferently, and the rest worse than any other conductor of eminence I have ever known'.[88] If this was Beecham's view in 1912 it seems strange that Phillips should have been asked to try to book him for the Covent Garden performances.

In his autobiography Beecham gave a full account of the events of 1912 and 1913, including the visit to Berlin (which was the first by any British orchestra), but at no point does he mention Phillips. This suggests that their association was short-lived, but whatever the circumstances, it is clear that for a time Phillips found himself at the very centre of British operatic and orchestral endeavour and during one of the most exciting periods in musical history. [89] As the country drew close to the catastrophe of the First World War Phillips found himself the possessor of flourishing music businesses in both Belfast and Derry, a promoter of concerts featuring some of the world's greatest stars, and with the experience of having worked for the most brilliant and imaginative young conductor on the musical scene.

OPERA MANAGER

The outbreak of the war severely limited the activities of the concert agency, but at this point his career took a new direction when he established his own opera company. More is known about the demise of this company than about its achievements thanks to the survival among the L'Estrange and Brett archive in the Public Record Office of Northern Ireland of a bundle of papers detailing the sorry state of its finances in 1918.[90] The period before 1914 saw a number of opera companies flourish and soon wither.[91] As has been noted, Thomas Beecham founded a company in 1910 largely underwritten by his father's wealth. Beecham was also able to bale out for a short time another company, the Denhof, which ran out of money in mid tour. Yet another short-lived company was the Harrison-Frewin (originally the Quinlan Company). The only truly successful company, although it too had many financial ups and downs, was that which bore the name of its founder, the Carl Rosa Opera Company. Established in 1875 by a German violinist and conductor it combined a London season with tours to the provinces and premiered many operas now part of the standard repertory. Following the founder's death in 1889 ownership passed to other hands and at one time there were three different touring companies, and in 1893 the title Royal was conferred by Queen Victoria. After the end of hostilities in 1918 the Carl Rosa Company absorbed a number of the other struggling companies including the Harrison-Frewin and Phillips's own, and it is to these transactions that the papers in the PRONI relate.

They disclose a financial tangle too complex to unravel here, but in essence it seems that Phillips had acquired the Harrison-Frewin Company in 1916 for £1,750. By March 1917 it was in debt to the sum of £1,317 12s10d. The H.B. Phillips Company then acquired the Harrison-Frewin Company from themselves as vendors 'by the allotment of 6000 fully paid up shares of 5/= each'. Phillips's partner, a Belfast businessman L.M. Ewart whose family fortune came from linen, put up much of the finance. Phillips ran the company as managing director, but the losses increased. The reasons were not hard to find, for, as the accountant brought in to untangle the financial mess noted, 'a large part of the loss incurred between June and December 1917 arose during the London season when business was practically at a standstill owing to Air Raids'. A financial statement drawn up in February 1918 showed that liabilities exceeded the value of assets by over £4,000. Phillips was entitled to draw a salary of £20 per week plus hotel and travelling expenses, and even though this was reduced to £10 the situation was parlous and it seems that Ewart wanted his money back. H.B. Phillips's concert agency was also in difficulty and owed money which it could not recover as many of the debtors were enemy subjects or out of the country and could not be contacted. The conclusion to the unhappy state of affairs was that in October 1918 the Carl Rosa Company acquired the Phillips and Harrison-Frewin companies, although Henry Phillips remained as artistic director. The Carl Rosa Company agreed to pay the outstanding balance of £3,000 to Ewart which it did in instalments of £100. In 1923, however, Phillips became the sole owner of the Carl Rosa Opera Company and he was to own and run it until his death more than a quarter of a century later.[92]

The period of Phillip's ownership of the Carl Rosa company deserves its own thorough study and this is not the place to attempt it, other than to observe that he eventually guided it to a period of great success when it provided most of the opera heard outside London. In the early years of Phillips's ownership it also supported a ballet company with his daughter as the principal dancer under the direction of the leading Russian ballerina Lydia Kyasht.[93] Without the efforts of the Carl Rosa Opera Company many places in Great Britain and Ireland would never have seen or heard a full-scale opera given by a professional company. Many fine singers and conductors made their reputations with the company, among whom was the great Australian soprano Joan Hammond. She has left an affectionate portrait of Phillips whom she came to know when the company was recovering from the loss of it entire stock of costumes and scenery in the London blitz.[94] Writing of the period when she joined the company she later recalled:

> Early in February 1942 I met H.B. Phillips, who was about to put his opera company, the Carl Rosa, on the road again. At a time of unrest and general insecurity, this must have been a big decision; but he was a man of enterprise and foresight. He was to be the sole means of giving the British people opera during the early war years. He was a gentleman in the best sense of the word, and I personally found him to be a man of his word. I enjoyed a friendship that lasted until the end of his life, and I learnt a great deal from this fine old man of the theatre.[95]

In an interview published in the *Daily Mail* in 1948,[96] the year in which he was made CBE in the King's birthday honours, H.B. Phillips looked back over the good times and the bad, 'the music famine years of World War I, through the touch-and-go early 'twenties into the boom years of World War II and after'. He recalled how one night they took £1 19s 0d gross, how costs were once £800 per week and takings only £300, how the war years had seen a booming demand for opera and in the years after advance bookings were counted in many thousands of pounds. He remembered how at one time special trains were laid on for the company but now15–20 tons of scenery had to be packed into seven trucks. Ever looking to the future he was planning to put on productions in cinemas to widen further access to opera for all.

Phillips was tireless in his efforts on behalf of the company – there was more than a grain of truth in his entry in *Who's who* which gave 'work' as his only recreation. The burden was shared by his wife Nettie who worked closely with him throughout this period. She continued as sole director after his death on 19 March 1950, but the optimism of only a few years earlier soon dissipated. Costs were rising at an alarming rate and the recently-established Arts Council made funding available for a time. But the opera world was changing, and the attention and funding shifted to permanent London-based companies where standards were higher. Nettie resigned in September 1957. The company struggled on for few more years until it was finally disbanded in September 1960. Mrs Phillips lived in retirement on the Isle of Wight until her death in 1969.

This remarkable couple who together did so much for the musical life of Britain and Ireland for over sixty years are remembered in a simple wooden plaque on the south wall of St Paul's Covent Garden, 'the actors' church', amid memorials to many of the great men and women of the stage. It bears the inscription:

Henry Bettesworth Phillips CBE 1866–1950
and his wife Annette 1881–1969

Owner-directors of the
Carl Rosa Opera Company

However, as this study has shown, Phillips deserves to be remembered for much more than his achievements as the owner of an opera company. Some of his greatest triumphs in another field are discussed in Chapter 2.

NOTES

1 Some of his newspaper obituaries give Kilkenny as his place of birth in common with his younger siblings. However his birth certificate records his birth at Athy Railway Station where his father served as stationmaster. He was presumably in the employ of the Great Western and Southern Railway which served both Athy and Kilkenny.

2 *Slater's Directory Ireland* (Dublin, 1870), under the entry for Kilkenny.

3 It is not known why Henry was given the unusual Christian name Bettesworth. None of his forebears is known to have had it, but a number of his grandchildren were so named. In later life his family knew him as Harry and his colleagues as HB.

4 After his death when his sons enrolled in school (see below) his profession was recorded as stationmaster which suggests that this had been his chief occupation.

5 *Slater's Directory Ireland* (1870), under the entry for Kilkenny.

6 Obituary notice for 'Mr H.B. Phillips' in the *Londonderry Sentinel* in its issue which covered the period 18 March–1 April 1950. A similar statement is made in the obituary in the *Derry Journal* of 22 March 1950.

7 PETER GALLOWAY, *The cathedrals of Ireland* (Belfast: Institute of Irish Studies, 1992), pp. 65-69.

8 JAMES B. LESLIE, *Derry clergy and parishes: being an account of the clergy of the Church of Ireland in the diocese of Derry, from the earliest period . . .* (Enniskillen: The Author, 1937), p. 42. Reprinted in *Clergy of Derry and Raphoe* (Belfast: Ulster Historical Foundation, 1999).

9 LESLIE, *Derry clergy*, pp. 23–25.

10 'Once in royal David's city' and 'There is a green hill far away' are two of the best known of her many hymns. VALERIE WALLACE, *Mrs Alexander: a life of the hymn-writer Cecil Frances Alexander 1818–1895* (Dublin: Lilliput Press, 1995), pp. 147-66 describes life in the Bishop's palace in Derry during this period.

11 W.H. GRINDLE, *Irish cathedral music: a history of music at the cathedrals of the Church of Ireland* (Belfast: Institute of Irish Studies, 1989*)*, p. 150.

12 MICHAEL HOEG, *The music of St Columb's Cathedral Londonderry* (Londonderry: [The Cathedral], 1979), p. 7.

13 GRINDLE, *Irish cathedral music*, pp. 114–15.

14 HOEG, *Music of St.Columb's*, p. 9.

15 Robert subsequently held the post of organist at St Nicholas's Galway, and from 1889 at Bangor Parish Church. I am grateful to his grandson Mr Ian Jones for information about this branch of the extended Phillips family. It is interesting to note that successive generations of the Jones family have been given the Christian name St John deriving from H.B. Phillips's father Henry St John Phillips.

16 *Londonderry Sentinel*, 29 December 1881. The performance was also reported in the *Musical Times*, 1 February 1882, p. 102, probably the first mention of his name in a national publication.

17 *Slater's Directory Ireland* (1870), under the entry for Londonderry.

18 'Foyle College Register' p. 19. I am grateful to Mr Alan Roberts of the Foyle College Old Boys' Association for supplying me with a transcription of the entry in the Register and with much useful information about the school's history.

19 Hime was born in Co Wicklow and educated at Portora Royal School Enniskillen. He entered Trinity College in 1858 at the age of 17 and graduated

in 1862. He was awarded his LLD in 1878. G.D. BURTCHAELL and T.U. SADLER, *Alumni Dublinenses*, new edition (Dublin: A. Thom, 1935), supplement, p. 56.

20 *Prospectus for Foyle College 1878* (Dublin printed, [1878]), p. 2. Copy in the Linen Hall Library Belfast.

21 In a copy of *Slater's Directory Ireland* in Belfast Central Library lacking a title page but from internal evidence dated ca. 1880.

22 *Slater's Directory Ireland* (1870), under the entry for Londonderry.

23 The *OED*, 2nd ed. under the entry for giant('s) strides (by which name the fly-pole was also known) defines it as 'a gymnastic apparatus, consisting of an upright pole with a revolving head, to which ropes are attached, by holding which, one is able to take gigantic strides round the pole'.

24 *Carmen Foyliense &c* [np, nd]. Copy in the British Library London B675y.

25 See BRIAN LACY, *Siege city: the story of Derry and Londonderry* (Belfast: Blackstaff Press, 1990), chapters 9 and 10.

26 The 'Foyle College Register', p. 19 states that he left on 1 November 1880, but this was later amended to 1882. His younger brother William entered the school in May 1880 prior to his eleventh birthday and left in December 1882. 'Register', p. 20.

27 *The north of Ireland (illustrated) up-to-date. Londonderry* (London: Robinson, [ca. 1895]), pp. 45-46.

28 Nuala McAllister has shown that by the 1830s there were already abundant sources of music and musical instruments in the city, provided both by settled firms and visiting suppliers from London, Dublin and Scotland, and this provision continued to grow in the course of the next half century. NUALA McALLISTER, 'Contradiction and diversity: the musical life of Derry in the 1830 decade', in *Derry and Londonderry: history & society: interdisciplinary essays on the history of an Irish County*, edited by GERARD O'BRIEN (Dublin: Geography Publications, 1999), pp. 465-95.

29 *Belfast and Province of Ulster Directory1892* [hereafter *BPUD*] (Belfast: Newsletter Office, 1892). Much of what can be learnt about Phillips's movements at this time is derived from street directories, but as a guide to dating they are often at best only approximate. The presence of an individual at a certain address might well reflect the position in the year previous to the date of publication, and conversely an individual might still be listed at an address after he had moved. Further, there may be internal inconsistencies between the information listed under the alphabetical list of names, the listing by streets, and the classification by trade or profession.

30 CYRIL EHRLICH, *The piano: a history*, rev. ed. (Oxford: Clarendon Press, 1990), p. 9. Erhlich estimates the world production of pianos in 1890 at 212,000. Twenty years later the figure was nearer 600,000 (p. 222).

31 It should be noted that the piano unlike every other instrument (with the exception of the organ and the harmonium) is not tuned by the player but requires the expert attention of a tuner. Hence the supplier of the instrument is usually assured of an ongoing connection with and continuing source of income from the purchaser.

32 ALISTAIR ROWAN, *The buildings of Ireland: north west Ulster, the counties of Londonderry, Donegal, Fermanagh and Tyrone* (Harmondsworth: Penguin Books, 1979), p. 389. The Guildhall was destroyed by fire in 1908 and rebuilt and reopened in 1912. The opening of the Millennium Forum in September 2001 looks set to challenge the supremacy of the Guildhall after more than a century.

33 *Londonderry Sentinel*, 10 October 1891.

34 Programmes for these two concerts are in the PRONI D3497/1.

35 *BPUD 1896.*

36 *BPUD 1899.*

37 30 Shipquay Street was built some time before 1873. A three-storey building of Georgian character the ground floor has recently been converted to a restaurant. ULSTER ARCHITECTURAL HERITAGE SOCIETY, *List of historic buildings, groups of buildings, areas of architectural importance in and near the city of Derry* (Belfast: UAHS, 1970), p. 23.

38 The *Belfast Newsletter* of 28 November 1899 advertised the forthcoming appearance of the 'Newland-Smith Trio and Party' at Mr H.B. Phillips Grand Evening Concert.

39 A programme of the concert is preserved in the Barrington Baker Collection in Belfast Central Library, vol. 1, fol.19.

40 LYN GALLAGHER, *The Grand Opera House Belfast* (Belfast: Blackstaff Press, 1995), pp. 2–3.

41 H.M. Prior, apothecary, Ferryquay Street is first listed in *BPUD 1877*. The firm traced its origins to 1765. Prior had served as head-assistant and later partner of the previous owner before becoming the sole proprietor. See the entry in *The industries of Ireland part 1 Belfast and the towns of the north* (London: Historical Publishing Co., 1891), p. 151, reprinted as *Industries of the north one hundred years ago* (Belfast: Friar's Bush Press, 1988).

42 I am grateful to Ms Bridget Palmer of the Library of the Royal Academy of Music for providing me with the details of Annette Prior's time there.

43 It is possible that Annette Prior also studied in Germany for a time but the evidence is late and from a source littered with errors. *Festival of Britain 1951 in Northern Ireland. Official souvenir handbook* (Belfast: H.R. Carter, [1951]), p. 73.

44 Belfast City Choral Society, season 1908-9. First concert, Ulster Hall 4 December 1908. Programme in the Concert Programme Collection, Belfast Central Library.

45 *Derry Journal*, 15 October 1909. Information supplied by Mr Nat McGlinchy.

46 NINETTE DE VALOIS, *Come dance with me: a memoir 1898–1956* (London: Hamish Hamilton, 1957), pp. 176 and 213. Among the productions she took part in with Sadler's Wells were *The Rake's Progress* (1935), *The Gods go A-Begging* (1936) and *The Nutcracker* (1937). See CYRIL W. BEAUMONT, *The Sadler's Wells Ballet* (London: C.W. Beaumont, 1946), pp. 49, 106, 108.

47 Before 1907 the sales of tickets for his Belfast concerts were handled by two existing Belfast firms, Cramer, Wood & Co. and Hart & Churchill.

48 MARCUS PATTON, *Central Belfast: an historical gazetteer* (Belfast: UAHS, 1993), p. 120. Although the entrance to the shop was in Bedford Street Patton lists the building under Donegall Square South where the entrance to the offices in the floors above is located. Phillips used either address at different times, sometimes combining both within the same advertisement. Older residents of the city will recall it for many years as the showrooms of the Workshops for the Blind. It now houses the premises of a building society, but in appearance is very little changed from Phillips's time.

49 PATTON, *Central Belfast*, pp. 112–13.

50 ERHLICH, *The piano*, pp. 98–104. The method evolved in the 1860s but it was not until 1895 that a proper legal framework was put in place.

51 The long-established Belfast firm of Cramer, Wood & Co. claimed to have introduced the system 'the superlative beneficial advantages of which need

nowadays no endorsement' to the city before 1891. See *The industries of Ireland part 1 Belfast and the towns of the north, p.105.*

52 Advertisement in the *BPUD 1908*, p. 6.

53 Advertisement in Phillips concert programme for 21 November 1913. Linen Hall Library Belfast Concert Programmes fol. 5, no. 2.

54 In *BPUD 1910* and *BPUD 1911* no. 6 Bedford Street is listed as Phillips's Gramophone Salon, but in the following year it is vacant and later became a milliners.

55 Advertisement in Phillips concert programme for 24 November 1909. Linen Hall Library Belfast Concert Programmes fol. 1, no. 6.

56 Linen Hall Library Belfast Concert Programmes fol. 1, no. 6.

57 CHRISTOPHER FIFIELD, *True artist and true friend: a biography of Hans Richter* (Oxford: Clarendon Press, 1993).

58 FIFIELD, *True artist*, pp. 334 and 339.

59 Programme in the Barrington Baker Papers, Belfast Central Library, vol. 2, fol. 73.

60 *The Northern Whig*, Wednesday 11 December 1907.

61 FIFIELD, *True artist*, p. 431.

62 Linen Hall Library Belfast Concert Programmes fol. 2, no. 3.

63 British Library Egerton Ms 3302. Percy Pitt papers, vol. 2, fol. 14. Richter's correspondence is in German, but the volume in the British Library contains an anonymous translation of most it. The translation of this item is numbered 248.

64 Linen Hall Library Belfast Concert Programmes fol. 3, no. 4.

65 Linen Hall Library Belfast Concert Programmes fol. 4, no. 4 and fol. 5, no. 4.

66 By a strange coincidence it was Richter's return to Vienna to make his last appearance there after his first visit to Ireland in 1899 which gave Thomas Beecham his first opportunity to conduct a major orchestra. His father, recently elected mayor of St Helen's, had booked the Hallé for a concert in celebration, but when it was announced that Richter was unavailable his son persuaded him to let him take over. The orchestra reluctantly agreed when threatened with replacement by an orchestra from London. FIFIELD, *True artist*, p. 334.

67 *Sir Thomas Beecham . . . a calendar of his concert and theatrical performances*, compiled by MAURICE PARKER ([Westcliff-on-Sea]: [Sir Thomas Beecham Society], 1985).

68 MICHAEL KENNEDY, *Portrait of Elgar* (London: OUP, 1968), p. 191.

69 Linen Hall Library Belfast Concert Programmes fol. 1, no. 2.

70 MICHAEL SCOTT, *The great Caruso* (London: Hamilton, 1988), pp. 231-32.

71 Linen Hall Library Belfast Concert Programmes fol. 1, no. 1.

72 Letter dated 8 April 1948 to his niece's husband Jack Hobson (Phillips Papers).

73 HERBERT JEFFERSON, *Viscount Pirrie of Belfast* (Belfast: Mullan, n.d.), pp. 98–104.

74 *Belfast Newsletter*, 14 September 1909.

75 *Belfast Newsletter*, 15 September 1909.

76 *Belfast Newsletter*, 16 September 1909.

77 MALCOM RUTHVEN, *Belfast Philharmonic Society 1874–1974: a short history* (Belfast: [The Society], 1974). The Philharmonic brought such celebrities as Bottesini (double bass), Paderewski (piano) and Percy Grainger (piano) to Belfast.

78 Opened in 1862 the Hall could accommodate 250 performers and an audience of 2000. PATTON, *Central Belfast*, p. 30. The initiatives which led to the building of the Ulster Hall and its subsequent impact on the musical life of the city

have recently been described by Roy Johnston in ' "Here we sit": the creation of the Ulster Hall', in *Music and British culture: essays in honour of Cyril Ehrlich*, edited by CHRISTINA BASHFORD and LEANNE LANGLEY (Oxford: OUP, 2000), pp. 213–32.

79 Linen Hall Library Belfast Concert Programmes fol. 4, no. 1.

80 *Beecham Calendar*, notes that the season actually began on 29 January.

81 *Beecham Calendar* records only orchestral concerts in Paris on 13 June (the Beecham Symphony Orchestra) and 23 June when Beecham conducted another orchestra.

82 *Beecham Calendar* records that the concerts took place on 16 and 21 December 1912. ALAN BLACKWOOD, *Sir Thomas Beecham: the man and the music* (London: Ebury, 1994), p. 58 describes the difficulties encountered on this visit when a rough sea crossing made many of the orchestra ill and there was a dispute of over payment for extra rehearsals.

83 British Library Egerton MS 3302. Percy Pitt Papers, vol. 2, fol. 73b.

84 FIFIELD, *True artist*, p. 441.

85 Richter wrote in German. The translation is in the Pitt Papers vol. 2, no. 301. It was Richter's thrift in using the back of Phillips's letter which has ensured its survival among the Pitt papers.

86 FIFIELD, *True artist*, p. 443.

87 FIFIELD, *True artist*, p. 334. Beecham was dismissive of most foreign conductors. In one of the acerbic comments for which he was famous he once said, 'Why do we in England engage at our concerts so many third-rate continental conductors when we have so many second-rate ones of our own?'

88 THOMAS BEECHAM, *A mingled chime: leaves from an autobiography* (London: Hutchinson, 1944), p. 34.

89 By late 1913 Donald Baylis had become the general manager of Beecham's opera company. It is possible that Baylis was the illegitimate son of Thomas's father Sir Joseph and an unacknowledged half-brother to Beecham. ALAN JEFFERSON, *Sir Thomas Beecham. A centenary tribute* (London: Macdonald and Jane's, 1979), pp. 128–29.

90 PRONI D1326/25/3

91 J.C. HANDBY, 'The Royal Carl Rosa Opera Company', *Hinrichsen's Musical Year Book*, vol. iv (1949–50), pp. 94-100 though brief provides one of the best accounts of this period in the history of opera in Britain.

92 ERIC WALTER WHITE, *The rise of English opera* (London: John Lehmann, 1951), p. 120.

93 L.J. DE BEKKER, *Black's dictionary of music & musicians . . . to 1924*, 2nd edition (London: A. & C. Black, 1924), p. 569.

94 WHITE, *Rise of English opera*, p. 166.

95 JOAN HAMMOND, *A voice, a life: autobiography* (London: Gollancz, 1970), p. 124.

96 CECIL WILSON, 'Grand old man of grand opera', *The Daily Mail*, 2 July 1948, p. 2.

'ALL THE WAY TO LONDONDERRY'

THE VISITS OF McCORMACK, KREISLER AND ROBESON

F ROM THE TIME HE WENT TO WORK FOR Thomas Beecham, Henry Bettesworth Phillips and his family lived in England, and it was there he died and is buried.[1] But this did not mean he abandoned his businesses in Northern Ireland.[2] The shop in Londonderry continued to flourish throughout his lifetime and long after, and many generations of Derry men and women looked to it as the chief source of music and musical instruments in the city. It had a distinctive appearance, claiming to have the largest plate-glass window in any shop in the British Isles. Measuring 158 inches by 136 inches the window was shattered in a drunken brawl between two sailors on the night of 16 May 1947.[3] The Belfast shop however had closed by 1925, although Phillips had sold it some years before to A.F. Downham who nevertheless continued to trade as 'H.B. Phillips Beethoven House'.[4] Perhaps overseeing the running of two branches of the business in Ireland while wrestling with the financial problems of his concert agency and opera business was too much for even the indefatigable Phillips. It is significant of the high reputation of the Phillips name that Downham retained it even though he had been in business under his own name for many years.[5]

George ffolliott Phillips and Arthur Phillips, Henry's younger brothers, ran the Derry shop but Henry kept a close watch on things from England.[6] Nowhere is this attentiveness better illustrated than in the events surrounding the visits to the city in 1935 and 1936 of three of the most celebrated artists of the day: John McCormack, Fritz

Kreisler and Paul Robeson. The survival of much of the correspondence and background documentation allows a detailed picture to emerge of the many complex issues to be decided when promoting a series of recitals involving artists of their stature. The London agent for the three artists was Harold Holt, and most of the correspondence was exchanged between him (or members of his staff) and Mr J. McAdam, Phillips's manager in Derry, although the correspondence is formally addressed to Phillips.

Harold Holt was the leading English concert agent of the time. Born in South Africa, qualified as a solicitor and the possessor of a private fortune, he was originally in partnership with Lionel Powell, but when the latter died suddenly leaving a mountain of debts Holt took over. Norman Lebrecht has written of him that he was 'tactful, imaginative and inherently good-natured, [he] could do business with anyone'.[7] It was Holt who formed the London Philharmonic Orchestra for Sir Thomas Beecham, and he had many of the top British and foreign artists on his books. After the Second World War he lost much of his zest for the music business and died in 1953 at the age of sixty-seven, but in the mid-1930s he was at the height of his powers and brought to his business a sharp eye for detail. Despite the fact that Phillips was on tour with the Carl Rosa Opera Company he too kept a careful watch on matters concerning his firm's side of the arrangements and occasionally intervened directly.

The opening concert in the series took place on Tuesday 8 October 1935 and featured the celebrated Irish tenor John McCormack. The first letter to have survived looks back to difficulties encountered in promoting the event, and makes clear that Holt had burnt his fingers in the pricing and advertising for the concert and was happy to place greater reliance on Phillips's local knowledge of audiences, venues and advertising for the two forthcoming concerts.[8]

E.W. Evennett handled most of the detail of these concerts on Holt's behalf. He had been with McCormack on his visit and would later tour with Robeson on his.

Harold Holt
3 Clifford Street
New Bond Street
London W.1.

17 October 1935

Messrs. H.B. Phillips
Beethoven House
Londonderry

Dear Sirs,

As a result of our experience at the McCormack concert it seems obvious that the prices were too high and so these must be adjusted for the next two concerts. I should be obliged, therefore, if you would kindly let me have your suggestions for repricing the house, but avoiding if possible making any great difference in the capacity figure.

Furthermore, I am now convinced that the expensive display advertising we did for the first concert did not pull its full weight, and that you are undoubtedly correct in your suggestion that you could handle this locally and get equally good results at a much cheaper expenditure; therefore I should be glad if you would kindly take on this matter and arrange the newspaper advertising for the remaining concerts. I should, however, like to receive from you a schedule of the suggested advertisements, and nearer the time to receive a proof for approval.

Yours faithfully,
[signed] E.W. Evennett
p.p. Harold Holt [9]

JOHN McCORMACK

Count John McCormack (the title was a Papal one conferred in 1928), was the most renowned Irish singer of his or indeed of any age. He was born in Athlone in 1884 and early in his career established a reputation as an opera singer appearing in a variety of roles with many

Best wishes from
Yours sincerely
John McCormack
My first visit to Derry
Oct. 4th 09.

This makes me feel very old!
It was a great joy to come
back to Derry again, and I
hope it wont be so long before
my next trip. Yours sincerely,
John McCormack
Oct. 4. 1932

John McCormack's two previous visits to Derry,
twenty-three years apart, were recorded in the autograph album
kept by a member of the Phillips family.

of the world's leading opera companies. After 1918, however, he concentrated more on concert performances, and although best remembered for his singing of Irish and popular songs, he was an assured performer of Handel, Mozart and German *Lieder*. McCormack had become an American citizen in 1919 but later returned to live in Ireland.

This was not John McCormack's first visited to Derry; he had sung there in 1909 and again in 1932. In promoting the 1935 concert Holt had taken a two column-wide display advertisement in the *Derry Journal* of 7 October announcing the concert as the 'Only appearance of the world's most famous tenor' and offering tickets, to be had from Beethoven House, at prices ranging from five shillings to 12s 6d. A similar, though smaller notice appeared in the *Londonderry Sentinel* of 5 October. McCormack's accompanist was Edward Schneider who had played for him for almost a quarter of a century, and they shared the platform with Betty Humby, a young concert pianist who later became the second wife of Sir Thomas Beecham. The *Derry Journal* ran a promotional piece in its issue of 4 October recalling the singer's last highly successful visit and suggesting that there would 'doubtless be an equally warm welcome when he returns next week – music lovers in the city and district will be anxious to hear the world's greatest singer of songs once more, to listen to his beautiful voice filling their municipal hall'.

But despite the promoter's best efforts the concert was not a sell-out, and in his review of the concert the reporter from the *Derry Journal* (9 October 1935) remarked that 'Last night's large audience was not quite so big as that of three years ago – there were quite a number of vacant seats in the higher-priced parts of the hall'. When this was put to McCormack after the concert the singer was the very model of diplomacy: 'he did not seem disappointed. He freely admitted that most people would find the front seats somewhat expensive. He was charmed with the Assembly Hall, saying that it was beautiful to sing in.' The *Londonderry Sentinel* was more forthright in its report in its issue of 10 October: 'The front seats were not filled, and Count McCormack expressed the view that the prices were too high.' The prices must certainly have seemed excessive in a city where unemployment was high and seats at an amateur performance of a Gilbert and Sullivan opera ranged from 6d to 1s 3d, and a night's dancing to the 'Rhythm Six Saxophone Dance Band' with special lighting effects and a running buffet could be had for 2s 0d each.[10]

McCormack's programme began with some songs by Handel, one of which was sung in Italian (prompting a citizen of that country who happened to be in the audience to remark to the man from the *Derry Journal* that 'the pronunciation here was splendid – better than his own'). Other songs in the first half included one by Rachmaninov. In the second half he gave the audience (what one suspects many of them had come to hear) a selection of Irish folk songs including 'Oft in the stilly night', 'She moved through the Fair', 'In the garden where the praties grow', and inevitably 'O Mary Dear', McCormack's own words to the tune 'The Londonderry Air'. He ended his recital, as was his custom, with a final group of popular songs:

> First, I give my audience the songs I love. Second, I give them the folksongs they ought to like and will like when they hear them often enough. Third, I give them the folksongs of my native land. Fourth, I give my audience the songs they want to hear, for such songs they have every right to expect. After all, the first duty of any artist to his public is to consider its tastes, and I have always done so.[11]

Shipquay Street, Londonderry in the 1930s.
Phillip's shop is on the right hand side beyond the Palace Cinema
where Fritz Kreisler went to see Mae West's latest movie.
AUTHOR'S COLLECTION

DERRY IN THE 1930S

Londonderry at the time of McCormack's visit in 1935 had changed greatly from the city Phillips had known as a schoolboy sixty years earlier. The relative prosperity of the last decades of the nineteenth century, later boosted by the manufacturing demands of the First World War, had by the 1920s given way to rapid economic decline.

By 1926 this decline had resulted in an unemployment total of some 28% of the working population. To a large degree this decline was part of the worldwide recession, but there was another factor – the partition of Ireland – which had had a particular effect on Derry's fortunes. The city had elected its first nationalist mayor in 1920, but this was followed by a period of considerable civil unrest and rioting in which many were killed or injured. The divisions between nationalist and unionist, Catholic and Protestant, were etched more deeply than ever. In December 1920 the Government of Ireland Act was passed setting up two parliaments in Ireland, in Dublin and Belfast. Ireland was divided, the six northern counties remaining part of the United Kingdom, the twenty-six southern and western counties now forming the Irish Free State. Derry, with nationalists comprising some 58% of the population and with a nationalist controlled council, found itself part of the new state of Northern Ireland and cut off from its natural hinterland of Donegal. This encouraged some businesses to relocate while others were forced out of business by the general recession. Many in the city expected that the promised boundary commission would rectify this position but its efforts came to nothing and, by 1923, thanks to changes in the voting system and the redrawing of electoral boundaries, the unionists were once again in control and the nationalists withdrew from municipal government for the next ten years.[12]

It was against this background of political and religious division and tension that McCormack found himself caught up in controversy. The issue of whether or not the British national anthem 'God save the King' should be sung at the conclusion of musical events went right to the heart of divisions in the city. Clearly there were those in the Guildhall audience that night in October 1935 who would have wished it sung, and equally there were those to whom the suggestion was anathema. At McCormack's concert in Newry on the previous Wednesday evening some members of the audience had taken it upon themselves to give voice to it causing no little outcry.[13] The *Londonderry Sentinel*, a strongly unionist newspaper (which would of course have been sympathetic to the anthem being sung) confined its remarks to a concise 'The National Anthem was omitted, and it was stated that this was customary at such concerts'. The staunchly nationalist newspaper the *Derry Journal*, which most emphatically would *not* have supported any attempt to sing it, went further in its reporting of the issue:

> There was apparently disappointment among a section of last night's
> audience at the fact that 'God Save the King' was not played or sung
> at the conclusion of the concert, as it had been at the Newry concert.
> When our representative passed a remark to the Count on the mat-
> ter, he said that it was not customary to have [it] at Harold Holt con-
> certs, even in London. An official connected with the organising of
> the concerts said that except where an orchestra was present and
> played it at the beginning of the concert the anthem was not heard.
> It will be recalled that 'God Save the King' was not played at the last
> McCormack concert in Derry.

This was not the first time in McCormack's career that the national anthem had been a source of controversy. Some sections of the
British press had been critical of his decision to become an American
citizen and renounce his allegiance to the King, and while on an
Australian tour in September 1920 he was attacked for not singing
the anthem at the conclusion of concerts. In Adelaide some of the
crowd began to sing it as he walked off the platform prompting
McCormack to cancel the remainder of the tour and return to
England. 'I am glad . . . to have suffered [ostracism] for being an
Irishman and an American . . .' he wrote at the time.[14]

If the *Sentinel* had dealt briefly with the matter of the national
anthem, leaving it to the *Journal* to make more of it, it showed no
reluctance in reporting the furore caused in nationalist circles by
McCormack's recently reported adverse comments on the tune chosen as the national anthem of the Irish Free State. The *Sentinel* (10
October 1935) quoted his views in a report which appeared under its
own headline:

> 'There is one worse tune than "A Soldier's Song", and that is the tune
> of the Italian Fascist hymn,' said Count John McCormack when
> interviewed in the City Hotel, where he stopped for the night in
> Londonderry before leaving for Belfast. The statement was made ...
> in reply to the direct question by a 'Sentinel' representative if he
> thought the tune of 'A Soldier's Song' the worst of any National
> Anthem. His reply was quick and decisive, and he further added that
> he could select at least one hundred tunes from Dr. Petrie's collection
> of old Irish airs which would be more suitable.[15] After humming
> a few notes . . . Count McCormack laughed and said – 'Oh! It is

dreadful. It is not what one would expect from a musical country like Ireland.'

The *Journal* (9 October 1935) reported the remarks rather more discreetly but was careful to add that the Count 'admitted, of course, the strong claims which the song had by reason of its patriotic associations.'[16]

The musical qualities of national anthems are of little concern to businessmen however: what matters is getting the arrangements right, keeping costs down and filling seats. Also preserved in the file of correspondence is an envelope on the back of which the advertising costs of McCormack's 1932 concert and that in October 1935 are compared.[17] The former totalled £6 6s 6d and the latter £16 15s 6d. These high costs and the failure to sell many of the more expensive seats had forced Holt to rethink his marketing strategy for the two remaining concerts. He had been encouraged in this by Henry Phillips himself. Writing from Birmingham where he was on tour with the Carl Rosa Opera Company, Phillips returned Holt's letter quoted above (which McAdam had sent to him for his consideration) with a letter of his own.

The Royal Carl Rosa Opera Company
Under the direction of H.B. Phillips

Please reply to – Prince of Wales Theatre
Birmingham

22 October 1935

J. McAdam, Esq.
Beethoven House
Londonderry

Dear Mr. McAdam,

I have written Holt a note to say had our advice been taken with regard to the prices for the McCormack concert the result would have been different and have also told him you are sending on particulars of the revised prices which I hope he will adopt.

Herewith I return Holt's letter and I think if you are looking after all the advertising by which they will save a considerable amount you should ask for an increased percentage.

Yours very truly,
[signed] Henry B Phillips[18]

Before Mr McAdam had had time to submit revised proposals Holt wrote again on 31 October asking for local information and advice about other venues:

I understand that when Count McCormack was in Londonderry you mentioned to him a concert hall in Coleraine.[19] Would you kindly send through to me particulars of this, and a plan of the seating. I am anxious to know the exact capacity of the Hall, and if you think it would be worth while to arrange a concert there for him.

How near is this to Ballymena, because there is a possibility of him giving a concert there early in the New Year, and if these two towns are very close together it simply means splitting the audience between the two towns. I understand the capacity of the Hall at Ballymena is 888 seats.[20]

McAdam's letter of 8 November dealt with both the revised prices for Derry and the advisability of giving a concert in Coleraine, and dutifully followed his employer's suggestion about a higher rate of commission.

Dear Sir,

In reply to your letter of the 17th October.

We now append below our suggested prices for the next two concerts, "Kreisler" and "Robeson".

			NETT	TAX.	GROSS	NET TOTALS
280	Ground Floor	10 Rows	8/–	1/–	9/–	112 0 0
364	do	13 :	6/9	9d	7/6	123 12 0
						[122. 17.0][21]
160	Upper Balcony		5/6	6d	6/–	44 0 0
			[5/3]	[9d]		[42 0 0]
152	Lower Balcony		4/–	6d	4/6	30 8 0
108	Platform		3/2	4d	3/6	17 2 0
						£327 0 0
						[324 7 0]

With regard to the advertising, which you now propose to place in our hands for the two concerts, we would estimate between £7 0s 0d and £10 0s 0d. It certainly won't exceed the latter figure, for each concert.

In view of the amount of work involved in these concerts we would suggest that the commission be increased to 10% (ten per cent) and would be glad if you would give this matter your consideration.

With reference to your letter of the 31st Oct. We herewith enclose letter and scale of charges for the Concert Hall at Coleraine, which you will note, is a considerably smaller capacity than the Hall at Ballymena. The distance between the two towns is only about 26 miles, and the bus time about 70 minutes, so there would be the possibility of splitting the audience.[22]

Harold Holt himself replied a few days later in courteous but emphatic terms:

The scale of charges now suggested by you for both the Kreisler and Robeson concerts in Londonderry are quite satisfactory, and we will be obliged if you will kindly put the printing of the tickets in hand at these prices. We will have the printing prepared for you and this will reach you in a few weeks' time.[23]

We note you propose spending between £7 and £10 for newspaper advertising for each of these concerts, and this is quite satisfactory; perhaps you would let us see a proof in due course.

With reference to your last paragraph, I am extremely sorry that I cannot see my way to increase the commission to 10%, as this is out of all proportion to the amount of money we are able to get into the house, and unless you feel you can look after the local arrangements at the usual Box Office commission of 5%, then I shall be reluctantly compelled to cancel the Londonderry concerts.

I might mention that 5% is the regular amount paid to all agents throughout the British Isles, and for Newry and Limerick.

Thank you for all the information in your letter regarding Coleraine, and I agree with you that it would not be a very wise move to arrange a concert there as well as in Ballymena.[24]

The prices McAdam suggested showed a considerable reduction on those charged for the McCormack concert; a range of 9s 0d to 3s 6d as against 12s 6d to 5s 0d, and if all were sold it would mean total box office takings of £324 7s 0d, as the amended copy of McAdam's letter of 8 November showed. But out of this of course were to be paid the costs of the hall, advertising and printing, travel expenses, and taxes, to say nothing of the artists' fees. At 5% Phillips might hope to make about £16 from the venture. If the tickets did not sell well, as in the case of the McCormack concert, then everyone stood to lose. As the later correspondence reveals, Holt was to become increasingly concerned about the sluggish sales of the tickets for the next concert. Holt's refusal to increase the commission probably came as no surprise to Phillips or McAdam, and in his reply dated 12 November McAdam graciously accepted the position: 'We regret that you cannot see your way to increase the commission to 10%, and in view of the explanation, we are quite prepared to carry on at the old rate, i.e. 5%'. [25]

In his next letter of 14 November Evennett expressed his satisfaction that things were going well and asked to see the schedule and a proof of the newspaper advertising.[26] When this had been furnished, another member of Holt's staff, H. Horton, wrote on 22 November with detailed comments on how the design might be improved.[27] Clearly nothing was being left to chance and five days later he was happy to confirm that all was now in order for the visit of the great violinist.[28]

FRITZ KREISLER

It has been written of Fritz Kreisler that 'In the entire history of violin playing there is probably no performer who has been more universally loved and admired. He appealed to the heart of his audience, not only by his virtuosity but by a quality that exuded a subtle vitality, humour, sweetness and pathos in an interfusion of tone, technique and communication.' [29]

Kreisler was born in Vienna in 1875, and began to play the violin when only four years old making his first public performance at the age of eight. By the time he was twelve he had already carried off all the prizes at the conservatoires in Vienna and Paris, and, still in knee breeches, undertook his first concert tour of America in 1888. On his return to Austria to complete his education he gave up music choosing instead to follow a career in medicine, but later thought better of it and returned to the concert platform in his twenty-first year.

No longer a child prodigy, he did not at once meet with success, but his performance of the Mendelssohn violin concerto in Berlin in

Publicity photograph of Fritz Kreisler inscribed
'To Mr Arthur Phillips in kind remembrance of F Kreisler Jan. 16. 1936'.

1899 confirmed him as a truly outstanding talent. Soon Kreisler was delighting audiences throughout the world, and in October 1904 he played in the Ulster Hall in Belfast in the Philharmonic Society's first concert of the season. The reporter from the *Belfast News Letter* in the issue of 15 October 1904 responded to his playing with enthusiasm. 'Herr Fritz Kreisler came to Belfast with a high reputation . . . and from his performance last night one would be hardly disposed to cavil at the exalted position thus assigned to him.'

He returned to Belfast in November 1910 (just a few weeks after he had given the first performance of Edward Elgar's violin concerto) to appear in one of Phillips's Subscription Concerts.[30] At the outbreak of war in 1914 he enlisted in the Austrian army and before long was wounded and invalided out. He went to live in America and for a time was out of favour for his continuing support of the Austrian cause. After the war he lived mostly in Berlin enjoying the adulation of music lovers throughout the world.

For many years it had been Kreisler's custom to include in his programmes short pieces which he attributed to minor eighteenth-century composers, but early in 1935 he publicly claimed them as his own. Not every critic was amused at having been taken in.[31] His Derry programme correctly identified them as his own compositions 'in the style of ...'. Kreisler later returned to America and became an American citizen. It was said of him that he used never to practice between performances.[32]

While everything seemed to be in place for the visit of the violinist on 16 January 1936, difficulties had arisen over the date for Paul Robeson's concert. A rapid exchange of letters took place proposing several different dates and causing no little confusion until at last, on 23 December 1935, it was agreed to risk putting him on on a Saturday night, 8 February 1936, for, as Evennett wrote, 'Paul Robeson, [is] one of the most popular attractions in the world; we find in other towns that one night is just as good as another where such a popular attraction is concerned.'[33]

There was also the matter of a suitable piano for Robeson's concert. Phillips, it will be recalled, had begun his career as piano tuner and dealer, and it would be reasonable to expect that his shop could provide one from its own stock. That was the expectation of the firm of Blüthner and Co Ltd of Wigmore Street London who wrote on 12 December asking the Derry shop to make available for the concert the 'Blüthner Grand Pianoforte' which was held 'on sale or return'.[34]

As Christmas 1935 drew near Holt began pressing for returns of the ticket sales and seeking assurances that everything possible was being done to promote both forthcoming concerts. Among the papers in the PRONI is a page torn from a cash ledger which lists the various outlets used to advertise the concerts, and these included: billposting, 500 circulars sent out by post, window cards in hotels, cafes and clubs, and advertisements carried by the local bus companies. But despite this, with the turn of the year Evennett began to worry about the slow sales and wrote on 7 January suggesting that spending on advertising should be increased to £15 from the agreed figure of £7-£10. Holt had already agreed (6 December 1935) to a slight reduction in prices for groups of students of fifteen or more.[35]

Although Kreisler's visit was barely a week away, it was not until 8 January 1936 that the world famous piano-manufacturing firm of Steinway and Sons wrote to Derry with detailed instructions about the piano for the concert. It is clear from the letter that Henry Phillips in London had attended to this matter personally. The letter, signed by Frank Usher of Steinway's Concert and Artist Department, is worth quoting at length for the information it contains about the preparation of the instrument:

> Mr. H.B. Phillips personally called upon us this morning and informed us that you have a Steinway 6 ft Grand available for Mr. Kreisler's recital. Upon enquiring of Messrs. Harold Holt as to whether this instrument would be suitable, they have entirely agreed. Therefore, on Mr. Phillips's suggestion, we would ask you kindly to supply the instrument for the recital, tuned to C 528, and charge us £2 2s 0d direct as agreed with Mr. Phillips.
>
> We enclose herewith a tuning fork of pitch C 528 for your use and shall be glad if you will kindly return it to us as soon as possible after the concert.

Phillips underscored these instructions to Mr McAdam in a letter of his own written and posted from London on the same day:

> Dear Mr McAdam
>
> I am sorry to hear you've been laid up & hope you will soon be alright. I've just seen Mr Usher at Steinways & while I was with him he rang up Holt who agreed to the (Colhouns) Steinway. Tuning fork is being sent to you today – it means the raising of the pitch so I expect it will need two or three tunings before it will stand in tune. See & have it perfect. You are to charge £2 2s 0d inclusive.

What about getting permission to use it?

Yours sincerely
[signed] H.B. Phillips

These two letters are of considerable interest for the light they throw on the problem of ensuring that a decent piano is available to the touring performer. Clearly it is impracticable to travel with a piano so the artist or the accompanist has to make do with whatever is provided at each venue. Often the best that can be hoped for is that sufficient attention has been paid to the preparation of the instrument which awaits the arrival of the musicians. In this instance Phillips made a point of calling with Steinways who sought Holt's agreement that the proposed instrument would be acceptable. It is significant that this instrument was not among Phillips's own stock but appears to have been privately owned. The reference in Phillips's letter to McAdam to the 'Colhouns Steinway', and his question about getting permission to use it bears this out. The Colhouns referred to are probably the same family who owned the *Londonderry Sentinel*, and Major Colhoun is known to have attended the concert in a complimentary seat.[36] Steinway's letter also gave instructions about the tuning of the piano and included a tuning fork to be used in this operation. This was done because the pitch was to be higher than that normally used in Britain, and Steinways could not have been sure that Phillips's tuner would have had one available.[37] The higher pitch would have ensured a more brilliant sound from the violin and represents the pitch with which Kreisler as a continental musician would have been more familiar. Kreisler, who was a friend of the Steinway family in America was known to prefer their pianos above all others.[38] Phillips was determined that the instrument would be properly prepared and warned McAdam that it would need a number of tunings before it was ready. 'See & have it perfect' he told McAdam underlining the words in his letter. Given the difficulties over finding a date for the Robeson concert, pressure from Holt to sell more tickets and now his employer writing with exacting instructions about the piano it is little wonder that poor Mr McAdam had 'been laid up'.

This commendable attention to detail displayed by Steinways and H.B. Phillips raises the question whether Kreisler could always expect such care to be taken on his behalf. Given the many venues he played in and the frequency with which he toured it is perhaps unlikely. He was known not to bother even slackening off his bow before putting it away, and, given his consummate skill, he probably could have played with any pitch or tuning he encountered on arrival at the concert hall. But he would no doubt have been pleased with the care taken to get everything as he wished it in Derry. Holt was probably less concerned with the details of pitch than with the poor sales of tickets. In Mr Evennett's letter of 10 January, written six days before the concert, the disappointment felt in London could no longer be hidden:

> Thank you for your letter of the 9th inst. enclosing returns of sales to date. These are certainly very poor for such a tremendous attraction and I cannot understand this lack of interest. However, now that you have been able to get some good write ups in the papers – which I have just been reading – and with the increased advertising you are arranging there may still be time to work up a capacity house. It will be terrible if the world's master violinist comes all the way to Londonderry for what I believe is his first visit to the town and there is a poor house.[39]

His pessimism is borne out by the 'Preliminary Concert Statement' supplied to Holt's agent, Mr Cooper, who accompanied Kreisler to Derry.[40]

Of the 1,173 seats on offer fewer than 50% had been sold. As might be expected the cheapest seats had sold best: 92% of the Lower Balcony (4s 6d) and 80% of the Platform (3s 6d). The Upper Balcony (6s 0d) had sales of 63%, but, as in the case of the McCormack concert, the expensive seats (though now reduced in price by almost 30%) had gone very badly: only 20% of the Ground Floor seats at 7s 6d and 21% of those at 6s 0d had been sold. The total value of the house was some £130 18s 9d, very far short of the hoped for return, and, at 5% commission, promising little more than £6 for Phillips.

Sales at the door improved the situation somewhat and the *Derry Journal* (17 January 1936) reported that the Hall 'was just about four-fifths full, but the organisers' agents, Messrs Phillips, considered an audience of some seven hundred was satisfactory in view of the high prices ruling in [a] portion of the hall'. The *Londonderry Sentinel* (18 January 1936) was vaguer and sought to excuse the empty seats, commenting that the audience 'was of surprisingly large dimensions in view of the prices and the many counter-attractions of modern times'.

Both newspapers agreed that it was a memorable occasion, and the *Journal* provided a vivid description of the player's manner:

> Without preparatory flourish, the Austrian violinist had plunged into Beethoven's Sonata in G major, No. 3, and very soon the coldness of the stage vanished; the whole hall became vibrant with colour. The man with the fiddle was quick to produce his credentials. This was Kreisler. Following the opening Beethoven piece, Kreisler had discarded his music, and from now on he played wholly from memory. During the change of themes in the "Poème" [by Ernest Chausson] when only the piano is heard, Kreisler's appearance of a nervous or highly-strung stance somehow gave one the impression of an inexperienced violinist waiting for an adjudicator to tell him to start. He held his violin by his side, flicked his gaze from audience to the ceiling, and with his other hand a couple of times brushed his hair as if it were coming down over his forehead. But it was grey hair, the grey hair of one who has been world-famous since the beginning of this century; and once the violin with precision was brought to his shoulder in time for resuming the theme the assurance of genius was back again.

Kreisler, who was accompanied by Charlton Keith (a noted pianist who was professor of piano at Trinity College, London), obliged the audience with a number of encores including his own arrangement of 'The Londonderry Air'.[41] The *Sentinel* doubtless took pleasure in recording that 'The concert ended on a memorable note, when the great violinist accompanied the singing of the National Anthem'. So much then for the assurances given at the McCormack concert that it was played only when an orchestra was present.

Kreisler gave interviews afterwards and both newspapers reported his views on music on the radio, something which many performers saw as a threat to their livelihoods:

> In addition to throwing thousands of people out of work [the *Sentinel* reported him as saying], and spoiling the sale of musical instruments it had a cheapening tendency. The man in the street does not appreciate what is thrown at him every hour of the day. Of course, it is worse in America, where you have symphony concerts interrupted to say that they are coming by courtesy of "Jones' Motor Company" for instance. In the old days if you wanted music you had to be able to play an instrument, but now just turn a knob. It killed the incentive to learn.[42]

Asked what he thought of Derry, he replied that he had not seen much of the city on account of the weather and had spent the afternoon at the pictures watching Mae West whose new film *Going to town* was showing at The Palace Cinema.[43] The *Journal* recorded his willingness to sign autographs for all who asked him and the *Sentinel* published a photograph of the violinist in the company of Charlton Keith, Arthur Phillips and Mr Cooper.

With the visit of Paul Robeson now imminent and the disappointing sales for the Kreisler concert adding to his concerns, Holt took the step of personally telegraphing Mr McAdam on 20 January[44] telling him to reduce the prices further. He repeated this instruction in a letter in which he expressed his hopes for a better turn out for the American singer:

> We have plenty of time yet to work up the interest in this concert, and I feel that a Saturday evening will be very good for Robeson, who has a big popular appeal. In fact he draws the radio, theatre and film public, so I think contrary to your suggestion he is more likely to empty the cinemas on that night than vice versa.[45]

McAdam wrote back assuring him that sales were going well and that he did not anticipate having to increase the spending on advertising.[46] Holt further asked him to invite the drama and film critics from the local press and to make sure that they all had tickets.[47] Holt knew that Robeson would appeal to a wider audience than music lovers and sought to maximise interest in his artist. He continued to press Phillips on the ticket sales and the Derry firm was true to its word in promising to get 'write ups' in the local press. On 25 January the *Londonderry Sentinel* carried a piece expressing the view that 'There is sure to be a packed house to hear Robeson, who, just back from Hollywood, is on his first concert tour of the British Isles.' The London people were pleased with this but less happy with the advertising, and Evennett wrote a detailed letter on 27 January setting out instructions on the location and layout of the advertisements.[48] So a series of letters which began with Holt asking the help and advice of the local agent and trusting his opinion, ends with Holt getting more and more involved with the smallest details.

But at last, on 6 February 1936, came a letter from Mr Evennett (who was staying at the Grand Central Hotel in Belfast) advising the people in Derry that Paul Robeson and he would be travelling on the

6.15pm train, arriving at 8.55pm, and asking the press to meet with them in their hotel at 9.30pm. As a final prompt to Phillips to do everything to ensure a good house he commented, 'We are sold out here for tonight and I hope it will be the same on Saturday.'[49] An event which at times seemed so fraught with difficulty that it would never take place was finally about to be realised.

PAUL ROBESON

Paul Robeson was indeed one of the most popular artists in the world and the most famous black American of his day. Born in Princeton, New Jersey, in 1898, the son of a former slave, he won a scholarship to Rutgers College (now University) and excelled both academically and on the sports field. He graduated in law from Columbia University, but finding his career impeded by racial discrimination he turned to singing and acting. He made his first film in 1923 and began a career as a concert singer in 1925. The following years saw him starring in *Show Boat, Porgy and Bess* and, with Peggy Ashcroft and Sybil Thorndike, in *Othello*.

Robeson's visit to Derry was the tenth stop on a tour of twenty-one cities and towns which had begun at the Royal Albert Hall London on 19 January and was to end in Bexhill on 22 March 1936. The Irish leg of the tour had already included Dublin, Cork, Limerick and Belfast. He shared the platform with Lisa Minghetti, whom Holt's press representative, in a release sent to Derry for use in publicity, fulsomely described as 'the famous Viennese violinist and a very beautiful woman as well, graceful, striking and Titian haired. She is the incarnation of the beauty and romance of Vienna and her playing brings the glamour of that city across the footlights wherever she goes'.[50] The third member of the party, Adolf Hallis, briefly described as 'the celebrated pianist' was a South African who later pioneered much contemporary music. Robeson's accompanist was his usual partner Lawrence Brown.

On this occasion the promoter's high hopes were not disappointed and there was a packed house for the concert. The *Derry Journal* estimated that the audience 'was the largest seen at a celebrity concert in the city in recent years. All parts of the floor and balcony were crowded, and the large number of seats arranged on the stage were all occupied as well', and this is borne out by photographs published in the

INTERNATIONAL CELEBRITY CONCERT

Director - HAROLD HOLT   SEASON 1935-36

SAT. FEB. 8 at 8   ASSEMBLY HALL
GUILDHALL, Londonderry

HAROLD HOLT announces Personal Appearance of

PAUL ROBESON
THE WORLD'S GREATEST NEGRO ACTOR VOCALIST

with **LAWRENCE BROWN** at the Piano

LISA MINGHETTI
THE FAMOUS VIENNESE VIOLINIST

and

ADOLPH HALLIS
THE CELEBRATED PIANIST

Blüthner Piano

Tickets   3/6   4/6   6/-   7/6   9/-

H. B. PHILLIPS, Beethoven House, Shipquay Street, LONDONDERRY

The poster advertising the visit of Paul Robeson
showing the ticket prices before Holt reduced them further in his
determination to ensure a sell out.

PHILLIPS PAPERS

Sentinel which show scarcely an empty seat anywhere. Was this the result of the lower prices, or was it, as both newspapers suggested, because Robeson was so well known to his audience through his appearances on screen and radio and his many recordings? Whatever the reason, the high expectations of the audience were not disappointed, and it delighted in his familiar programme of Negro spirituals: 'Swing Low, Sweet Chariot', 'Poor Old Joe' and others; some Russian and English folksongs; the theme from the film *Sanders of the River* which had just been released and in which he had starred, and yet more spirituals. His encores inevitably ended with 'Ol' Man River', and he alone among the three visiting artists did not perform 'The Londonderry Air'. On this occasion too the concert concluded with the national anthem.

Publicity photograph of Paul Robeson.
Inscribed for Arthur Phillips 'with such pleasant memories of "Derry"
all [the] best & thanks. Feb, 8, 1936'

PHILLIPS PAPERS

POSTLUDE

There remained only the accounts to be settled, which Phillips did with exemplary efficiency. A copy of the balance sheet which Phillips prepared for Holt is preserved [51] and shows that in all 1,094 seats were sold realising a total of £233 2s 3d. In addition 619 programmes were sold at 6d each producing an income of £15 9s 6d. Phillips's outgoings were listed, and they serve as a reminder of the many details to which the local agent had to attend:

To D. Irvine Ltd.		
Printing Tickets etc	2 18 2	
D. Allen & Sons		
Bill Posting	4 4 8	
Standard		
Adv	4 4 6	
Journal		
Adv	3 16 6	
Sentinel		
Adv	6 4 0	
Peoples Press [52]		
Adv	0 12 0	
Attendants		
Pay x 5 Entrances	1 10 0	
Caretaker Guildhall	1 0 0	
Numbering seats etc	1 5 0	
Addressing & Posting	2 17 6	
252 @ 1½ 625 @ ½		
Post. Telegs. Phones	1 12 6	
Piano Hire	1 10 0	
Total	31 16 10	

Phillips retained the agreed commission of 5% of the ticket sales (£11 13s 2d), and one half-penny for each programme sold (£1 5s 9d) which meant that for all his efforts in promoting the concert his total return was £12 18s 11d. Holt's share was £203 16s 0d. [53]

Holt's accountant wrote to thank Phillips on 14 February. The letter reveals that, contrary to what had been agreed, the Blüthner piano was not after all used to accompany Robeson, rather the Steinway which had served Kreisler did service for him also. It seems rather hard to blame Blüthners for the poor condition of the piano which was after all in Phillips's stock and which Phillips was agent for. Did Phillips perhaps decide to stick with the Steinway to save the trouble and cost of transporting another piano to the concert hall and having it prepared? It is noteworthy that he charged only £1 10s 0d for the hire of it against the two guineas agreed with Steinway for the earlier concert.

Harold Holt
3 Clifford Street
New Bond Street
14 February 1936

Messrs. H.B. Phillips
Beethoven House
Londonderry

Dear Sirs,

I acknowledge with thanks your letter of February 12th, with enclosed detailed statement of receipts and expenditure for the ROBESON concert on February 8th. The account is all in order and I have pleasure in enclosing official receipt for the full amount of £203 16 0d, this being £173 16s 0d. received by cheque and £30 cash advanced to Mr. Evennett, as I have retained the receipt which he gave you.

   Thank you for your separate letter regarding the question of the piano, and your charge for the Steinway is, of course, in order. When I receive from Blüthners their account for the piano which was supplied by them I shall return it, pointing out that the piano delivered was absolutely useless from the point of view of solo work.

Yours faithfully,
[signed] J.B. Easton
Accountant
p.p. Harold Holt[54]

So one of the finest series of concerts ever put on in Londonderry was brought to a satisfactory conclusion. Nothing like it was seen in the city again. McCormack's career was in any case almost at an end and he retired from the concert platform in 1938, although he did make a number of appearances at Red Cross charity concerts during the Second World War. He died in 1945. Fritz Kreisler continued to

Harold Holt's receipt for the final revenue from Robeson's concert –
the grand sum of two hundred and three pounds and sixteen shillings.

PHILLIPS PAPERS

delight audiences for many more years. He moved to America and became an American citizen. In 1941 he was knocked down while crossing the street in New York and badly injured. Although he recovered he gave up playing after the 1949–50 season and sold his magnificent collection of violins. He died in 1962. Paul Robeson, by far the youngest of the three, fell from favour with the American public when, after a visit to the Soviet Union, he became an active apologist for communism. For a time his passport was withdrawn. Later however he won back the respect and admiration of many and travelled widely, working on behalf of a variety of charitable causes. He died in January 1976.

The school song which as a boy Henry Bettesworth Phillips learned to sing at Foyle College contained the inspirational lines:

> Then shirk, lads, no work, lads,
> But strive with might and main.

They might serve as a fitting epitaph for the man who, together with his wife, worked tirelessly for sixty years in the promotion of music and musicians in these islands.

NOTES

1   His funeral took place at Golders Green Crematorium on Friday 24 March. *The Times*, 25 March 1950.
2   In *BPUD 1909* and *BPUD 1910* Phillips's residential address was listed as 15 Rosetta Avenue Belfast, but thereafter the address was occupied by someone else which suggests that Phillips may have moved to London in 1911.
3   *Londonderry Sentinel*, 17 May 1947. The cost of replacement was put at £111 15s 8d.
4   An advertisement in the programme of the Belfast Musical Competitions, Ulster Hall, 21–24 April 1920 names Downham as the proprietor. Copy in Concert Programme Collection, Belfast Central Library.
5   A.F. Downham is first listed *BPUD 1900* as a music teacher at 7 North Street, Belfast and thereafter as owner of piano and organ showrooms at a number of different addresses. In *BPUD 1906* his premises in Talbot Street (one of three addresses listed in that year) are described as a 'pianoforte factory'. *BPUD 1926* lists the Bedford Street premises as vacant.
6   Another of Henry's brothers, William Lawless Phillips, was Assistant Town Clerk of Derry at this time.
7   NORMAN LEBRECHT, *When the music stops: managers, maestros and the corporate murder of classical music* (London: Simon & Schuster, 1996), p. 82.
8   The letters and other documents quoted are shared between the PRONI (D3497/1) and the Phillips family. Those in the PRONI are quoted by permission of the Deputy Keeper. Obvious errors in spelling or punctuation are silently corrected and monetary values are given in a standard form.
9   PRONI.
10 Advertisements in the *Derry Journal*, 7 February 1936.
11 Quoted in NIGEL DOUGLAS, *More legendary voices* (London: Deutsch, 1994), p. 145.
12 This period in Derry's history is dealt with in BRIAN LACY, *Siege city: the story of Derry and Londonderry* (Belfast: Blackstaff Press, 1990), pp. 221–37, and BRIAN MITCHELL, *Derry: a city invincible* (Eglinton, Co. Londonderry: Grocers' Hall Press, 1990), pp. 77–81.
13 *Derry Journal*, 7 October 1935 reported that 'As the strains of the music floated through the hall, Catholic and Nationalist members of the gathering remained seated or vainly attempted to make their way from the building, while some of them endeavoured to make a protest, but their efforts were overwhelmed by the volume of the singing by the Unionist section.'
14 Quoted in GORDON LEDBETTER, *The great Irish tenor* (London: Duckworth, 1977), p. 103.
15 George Petrie (1790–1866) in addition to his work as a painter and archaeologist collected many Irish airs which he published as the *Ancient music of Ireland* in 1855. 'The Londonderry Air' was first set down in this collection. A three-volume edition of the collection arranged by Charles Villiers Stanford was published in 1905.
16 The song 'Amthran na bhFiann' had been adopted as the national anthem in 1926. The music is by Patrick Heaney and Peadar Kearney who also wrote the words. The steps by which it was adopted as the national anthem and the tensions which it and the British national anthem provoked are examined in EWAN MORRIS, ' "God save the king" versus "The soldier's song": the 1929 Trinity College national anthem dispute and the politics of the Irish Free State', *Irish Historical Studies*, xxxi, no.121 (May 1998), pp. 72–90.

17 PRONI.

18 PRONI.

19 The Town Hall, built in 1859, with the addition of a large public hall in 1902.
    See ALISTAIR ROWAN, *The buildings of Ireland: North West Ulster*
    (Harmondsworth: Penguin Books, 1979), p. 20.

20 Probably the Town Hall opened in 1928.

21 The figures in square brackets are corrections written in manuscript on the car-
    bon copy of the original. H. Horton, one of Holt's staff, wrote on 14
    November (PRONI) pointing out the errors in the arithmetic in McAdam's
    schedule who then amended his copy of his letter.

22 PRONI.

23 i.e the printing of the programme, a single version of which usually served for
    all the concerts on a tour. The programmes were printed by Vail, a London
    printer who specialised in concert programmes.

24 Letter dated 11 November 1935 PRONI.

25 PRONI.

26 PRONI.

27 PRONI.

28 Letter of 27 November 1935 PRONI.

29 MARGARET CAMPBELL, *The great violinists* (London: Granada, 1980), p. 117.

30 Linen Hall Library Belfast Concert Programmes fol. 2, no. 2. This was part of a
    tour which covered Dublin on Thursday 24 November, Belfast on Friday 25th
    and Cork the following day.

31 A full account is given in AMY BIANCOLLI, *Fritz Kreisler: love's sorrow, love's joy*
    (Portland, Oregon: Amadeus Press, 1998), chpt. 7.

32 F.W. GAISBERG, *Music on record* (London: Robert Hale, 1946), p. 203. 'He of
    all the violin virtuosos rarely touches his instrument from one concert to the
    next. It is his boast that he does not practice because he declines to be a slave to
    his instrument'.

33 PRONI.

34 Phillips Papers.

35 PRONI.

36 Retained among the Phillips Papers is the 'book' for the Kreisler concert,
    a ledger in which the sale of tickets was recorded noting the name of the
    purchaser and seat(s) bought. Major Colhoun was allocated 3 free seats in
    Row D alongside the Duchess of Abercorn and her party (7 seats). Captain
    Herdman, a mill owner, had 4 seats in the same row. The book for the
    Robeson concert also survives.

37 It is usual today to express pitch in relation to A rather than C. Standard pitch
    in Britain is A = 440hz, C528 is equivalent to A = 442hz. I am very grateful to
    Mr Ulrich Gerhartz of Steinway and Sons for much invaluable information on
    this matter. He estimates that it would take a proficient tuner at least two
    hours to raise the pitch on a grand piano, but warns that if it were done badly
    the results would be disastrous for the players. Similar care would have to be
    taken to lower the pitch afterwards.

38 LOUIS P. LOCHNER, *Fritz Kreisler* (London: Rockcliff, 1951), pp. 341–2.

39 PRONI.

40 PRONI.

41 Kreisler is said to have given the first performance of his arrangement of 'The
    Londonderry Air' when he played it for Lloyd George on the day when the lat-
    ter had agreed the treaty for the Irish Free State with De Valera. A. CRAIG BELL,
    Fritz Kreisler remembered. A tribute (Braunton, Devon: Merlin, 1992), p. 22.

42 Kreisler did not overcome his opposition to the radio until July 1944 when he broadcast for the first time. 'I avoid the radio because I do not like the idea of being turned on and off like an electric light' he was once reported as saying. BELL, *Fritz Kreisler*, p. 33.

43 *Derry Journal*, 13 January 1936. The Palace Cinema was located next door to Beethoven House and Phillips owned a share in it.

44 Phillips Papers.

45 Phillips Papers. Holt could have saved himself the expense of the telegram as the lines were down between Belfast and Derry and it had to be forwarded by post arriving the same day as his letter.

46 Letter dated 21 January 1936 Phillips Papers.

47 Letter dated 22 January 1936 Phillips Papers.

48 Phillips Papers.

49 Phillips Papers.

50 Phillips Papers.

51 Phillips Papers.

52 *The People's Press, Donegal, Derry & Tyrone News*, which began publication in Lifford in 1931.

53 Holt of course would have to meet all the artists' expenses. It is interesting that the balance sheet contains no entry for the hire of Guildhall. Possibly this was a cost which Holt met directly.

54 Phillips Papers.